P9-CNE-704

Shaker Children

True Stories and Crafts • 2 Biographies and 30 Activities

Kathleen Thorne-Thomsen

Library of Congress Cataloging-in-Publication Data

Thorne-Thomsen, Kathleen.
Shaker Children / Kathleen Thorne-Thomsen.—1st ed.
p. cm.
Includes bibliographical references.
Summary: Describes the Shaker lifestyle through true stories of Nicholas Briggs and Anita Potter, two chidren who lived with them, one in the 1850s, and the other in the 1920s.
IBSN 1-55652-250-9 : $15.95
1. Briggs, Nicholas. 2. Potter, Anita. 3. Shakers—New Hampshire—Canterbury—Biography—Juvenile literature. 4. Children—New Hamphire—Canterbury—Biography—Juvenile literature. 5. Children—Massachusetts—Hancock—Biography—Juvenile literature. 6. Shakers—Massachusetts—Hancock—Biography—Juvenile literature. 7. Decorative arts, Shaker—Juvenile literature. [1. Briggs, Nicholas. 2. Potter, Anita. 3. Shakers. 4. Decorative arts.]
I. Title.
BX9791.T48 1996
289'.8—dc20

First edition
Published by Chicago Review Press, Incorporated
814 North Franklin Street
Chicago, Illinois 60610

Shaker Children
was inspired by my teacher and friend at the Institute of Design,
E. Ray Pearson, and is dedicated to his memory.

My special appreciation to
John Runnette,
David Duncan, Anita Potter Thorpe, Andrew Vadnais, and Stephen Miller.
I gratefully acknowledge help from: Graham and James Pulliam, Amy Teschner,
Linda Matthews, Joan Sommers, Richard Dabrowski, Julie Rockefeller,
Hank and Annie Gibbons, Maggie Kaufman, Lee Estes, Alicia Wilson Mulliken,
Linda Duncan, Hannah and Richard Wood, Marsha and Ed Nunn,
Brother Arnold Hadd, Sister Frances Carr, Renée Fox, Virginia McKewen,
June Sprigg Tooley, Linda Brownridge, and Jill Herz Hainz.

Shaker Children
Designed and composed by Kathleen Thorne-Thomsen
in Adobe Garamond and BauHaus with Kindergarten heads using
QuarkXPress 3.31r5 version for Macintosh
Printed by Wm. C. Brown Communications, Inc.

The road to Hancock Shaker Village

Contents

Biographies

Activities

Hancock Shaker Family, 1925

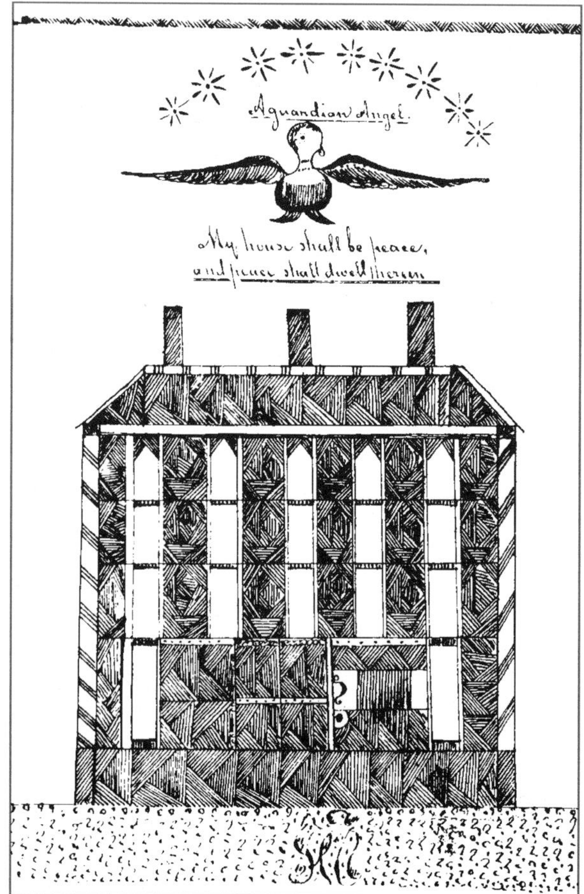

Shaker drawing.

The Shakers

The Shakers are a group of people who live together communally, sharing ideas, work, and property. Their real name is the United Society of Believers, but they are usually called Shakers because of the energetic dancing they did during worship services long ago.

Organized during Revolutionary War times, the Shakers are the oldest and most successful American commune. Following the principals of simplicity, order, perfection, cleanliness, health, and thrift taught by their founder and beloved leader, Mother Ann Lee, they want to live the perfect life in every way.

By 1850 there were five thousand Shakers living in eighteen self-sufficent villages that were so productive they were able to sell food, seeds, furniture, clothing, and fancywork to the world's people to supplement their income. Many of the everyday objects they made years ago are today considered to be so beautiful that they are important parts of museum collections.

Since the Shakers did not marry, it grew harder and harder for them over time to attract new members. Sadly, the numbers of Shakers declined, and by 1900 there were only a few hundred sisters and a handful of brothers. Today all of the Shaker villages except one have been closed. There are a handful of remaining Shakers living in the village at Sabbathday Lake, Maine.

Biographies

These are the stories of two real Shaker children: a boy, Nicholas Briggs, who lived with the family at Canterbury, New Hampshire, in 1852 when the Shakers were at their peak, and a girl, Anita Potter, who lived with the family at Hancock, Massachusetts, in the mid 1920s when Shaker membership was declining. Although the Shaker lifestyle changed dramatically between the two time periods, each child learned the Shaker devotion to craftsmanship and the simple beauty the Shakers found when they "put their hands to work and their hearts to God." Both children eventually left the Shakers, Nicholas after over forty years and Anita after four years. Each took a genuine love for the Shakers with them.

Shaker cat Theodore Roosevelt Chickenhouse and Shaker girl.

Nicholas Briggs

A Year in a Shaker Boy's Life

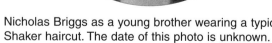

Nicholas Briggs as a young brother wearing a typical Shaker haircut. The date of this photo is unknown.

Summer 1852

The wagon slowed to a stop at the top of a hill. Ten-year-old Nicholas Briggs leaned over the side and looked out at a cluster of solidly constructed frame buildings standing in orderly fashion on the next hilltop. The village looked white and stark in the hot July sun.

The events that brought Nicholas to view Holy Ground, the Shaker village near Canterbury, New Hampshire, for the first time, began with his father's death. His mother was left with three children to care for: a baby, eight-year-old Julia, and Nicholas. It was hard for a single mother to support a family, and Mrs. Briggs would not accept charity from her friends and relatives.

One night she gathered her children around her and told them they were going on a train trip.

"We'll stay in a farm village that belongs to the United Society of Shakers," said Mother.

Nicholas wondered who the Society of Shakers were but he did not ask any questions. Mother looked sad and worried. How he wished Father could still be with them.

A few days later, on a hot July morning, the Briggs family boarded a train in Providence, Rhode Island, and began their journey into a new life.

They arrived at the lonesome Canterbury station in the late afternoon. The Shaker village was eight miles from the station, and Mrs. Briggs had no choice but to pay the mail carrier a fee to take them there. The horses were tired and the mail wagon bumped over potholes in the country road, making the trip slow and hot. Worst of all, the driver did not speak well of the Shakers. Nicholas climbed forward from the back of the wagon to hear what the adults said.

Early view of Canterbury Shaker Village from the south, showing the Church Family buildings.

Mary Whitcher.

"Shakers separate themselves from the rest of us, Mrs. Briggs. They call us *world's people.* It's like — we're not good enough for them.

"They don't allow marriage," the mailman continued. "Men and women are separated from each other, but they all live together in houses big enough to be hotels. If you cut one in two — straight down the middle — you'd have two identical pieces with the same doors, rooms, and staircases on each side. One half is for men and one half for women. It's peculiar for them to live that way."

Nicholas saw the worried look on his mother's face.

"You have children, Mrs. Briggs. When families go to live with the Shakers the children are taken from their parents and raised away from them. I don't think it's right to break up natural families."

Now Nicholas had a worried look on his face, too.

The wagon hit a big hole and the mail carrier stopped to catch his breath. "The Shakers believe that men and women are absolutely equal and they give women an equal say in everything they do. Can you imagine that! No one thinks that way!"

Nicholas leaned back against the side of the wagon and speculated about the Shakers. What would they be like? What would a house big enough to be a hotel look like? Would living with the Shakers mean he wouldn't see his mother anymore?

The Briggs family stood, hot, dusty, and tired, on the porch of a small building marked "Trustee's Office." A woman with a friendly smile dressed in quaint, old-fashioned style opened the door.

"Welcome. I am Mary Whitcher and you must be Mrs. Briggs. What lovely children. They must be hungry. I will bring some supper. *Yea?*"

Mary Whitcher set a feast of toast soaked in real cream, chunky warm applesauce, and delicious apple pie and cheese before the hungry Briggs family. After supper Nicholas was taken to play in the fields with a friendly Shaker brother. He was happy to be well fed and away from the crowded, noisy city.

At dusk, Mary Whitcher showed the Briggs family to a guest room in the hotel-size dwelling house. The room was furnished in a simple style. It was very pleasant, but did not remind Nicholas even remotely of home. The floor was painted a lively yellow, further brightened by colorful rag rugs placed in front of two bumpy, wide beds. Four straight-backed chairs with ribbon-woven seats were lined up against a wall. Above them were pegs holding a broom, clothes brushes, and a small mirror. Mary proudly told them everything in the room was Shaker-made.

Nicholas was up and dressed for breakfast before his family. He found Mary Whitcher in the hall.

"Please tell me about the Shakers," he asked shyly.

Mary smiled. "Shakers are religious people who lead a *communal life*. Communal means we own everything together. We are like one big family with more than one hundred members. In fact, we call each other *brother* and *sister*. Shaker families join together in villages. Our village, Holy Ground, has two families: the Church Family and the North Family. Each is governed by *elders*, two men and two women who share leadership responsibilities. And each family has *trustees* who take care of family business. I am a trustee for the Church Family, Nicholas.

"We are more than five thousand in number, living in eighteen villages in eight states. I am proud to be a Shaker, Nicholas. We live our religion by putting our hands to work and our hearts to God. That's why the garden seeds, medicinal herbs, applesauce, baskets, cloth, brooms, and chairs we sell to the people of the *world* are superior to all others.

Bird's-eye view of a Shaker room.

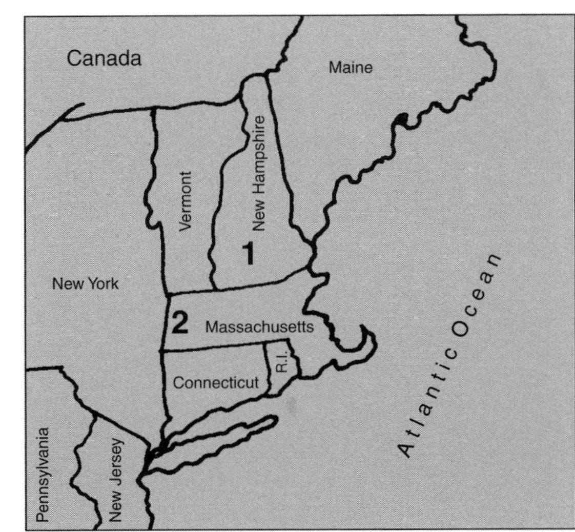

1: Canterbury Shaker Village.
2: Hancock Shaker Village.

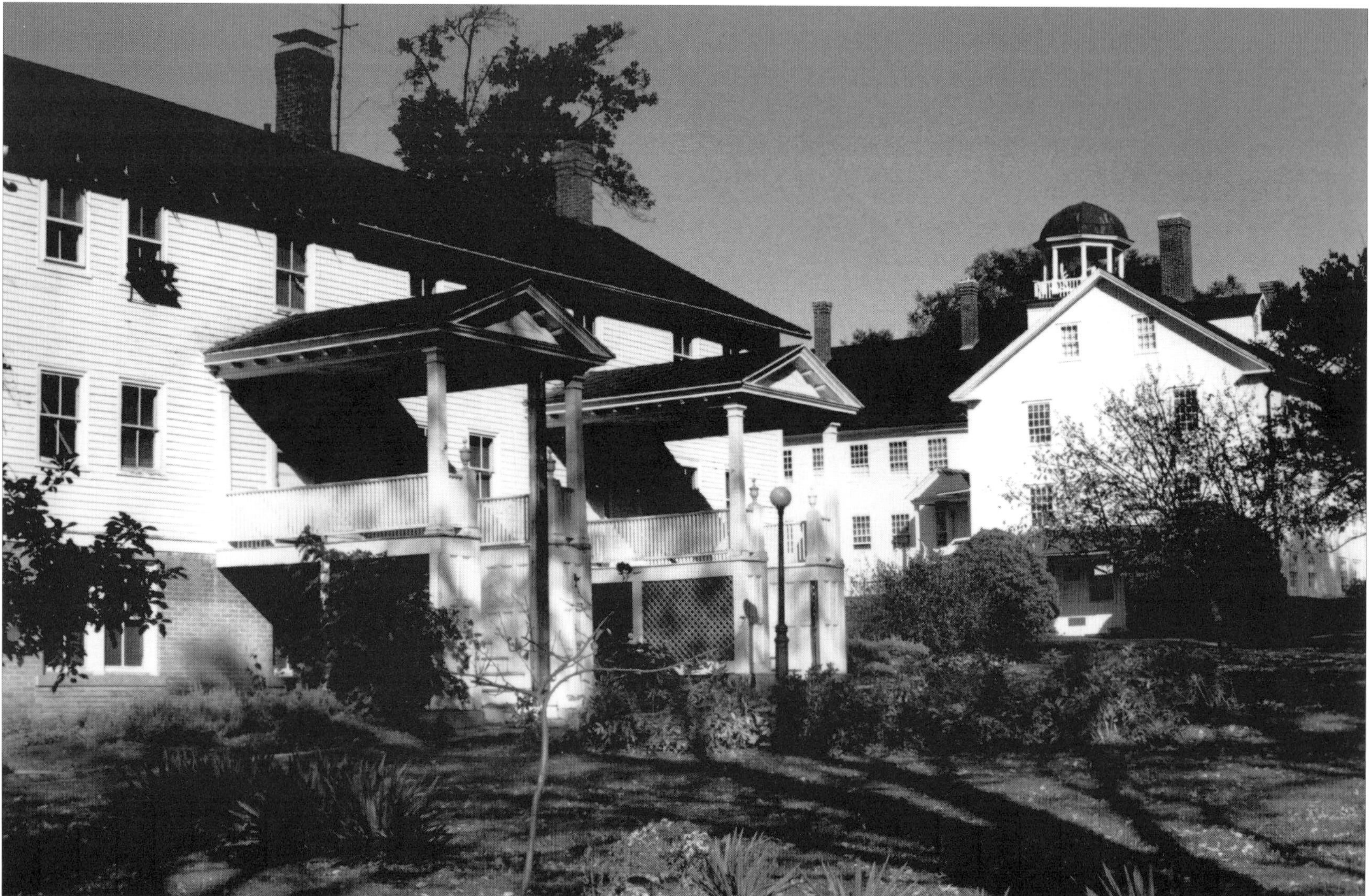

View of Canterbury dwelling house showing separate entrances for brothers and sisters.

The Shakers often moved buildings from place to place. The Creamery, shown above, now stands where the Boy's House once stood.

"You will be leaving the Church Family today to live with the North Family, where all newcomers to Holy Ground must live. I will miss you, Nicholas."

A Shaker brother came in a wagon after breakfast and moved the Briggs family to the North Family dwelling house. Mrs. Briggs left Nicholas outside to roam around the farm. He played for a long time in a hay field and then helped the Shaker sisters pick berries. He was happy. Mary Whitcher, the Shaker he knew best, was a kind lady. Shaker food was delicious and plentiful. He was growing accustomed to the strange Shaker way of saying *yea* for yes and *nay* for no. He hoped the Shakers would continue to allow his family to stay together. If they did, he would like living here.

During the next week Mrs. Briggs studied Shakerism and the family remained together. Finally, she told her children she did not see any reason why they should not join this community of loving people. But there was one problem. There were no children living with the North Family. Nicholas and his sister must be sent to live with the other children at the Church Family.

Tears ran down Julia's cheeks. Nicholas felt a lump in his throat.

"Children, please. I did not agree to this proposal at first, but the kindly Shaker sisters promised we will be able to see each other as often as we want, and so I gave my consent. Julia and Nicholas, you will go to live with the Church Family. The baby and I will remain with the North Family where I will work as a nurse in the infirmary."

Nicholas felt fear return to him twofold. The mail carrier had been right. He was to be on his own, separated from his family, after living only one week with the Shakers. He wanted to cry and tell his mother he would not go to live with the Church Family, but the decision was made and he had to obey her wishes.

On Saturday morning, the book Nicholas had brought with him from the world was taken away from him and he was picked up by Andrew, the boys'

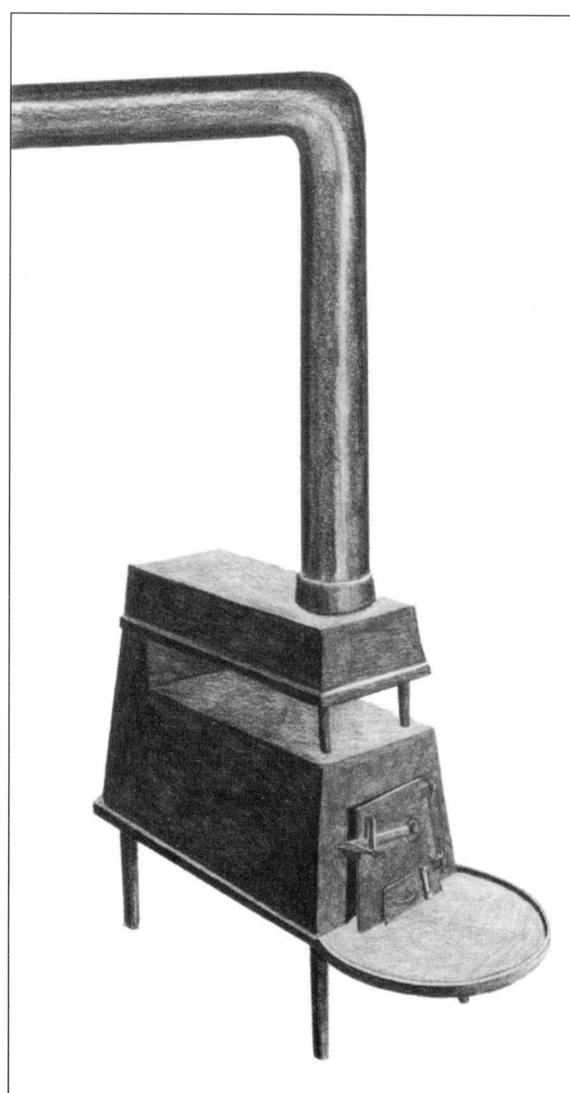
Shaker-made wood-burning stove.

caretaker, who immediately began instructing him on becoming a Shaker boy. They entered a large room furnished only with a long, straight row of chairs. Andrew called it the *Boys' Shop*. "This room is divided by an imaginary line, half for the younger boys and half for the older boys," he said. "There's one chair for every boy who lives here. You will sit with the older boys in the chair that is eighth in line."

Nicholas was delighted to be considered an older boy.

"You must keep your chair exactly where you find it," Andrew continued. "Shakers have a place for everything, and keep everything in its place. Because we believe we are living in heaven right here on earth, everything in our village is kept in perfect, heavenly order."

Nicholas studied the room. At one end was a bench and a bookcase full of books. A large wood-burning stove, a sink with running water, and the chairs were the only other things in the room. How he longed to have his own familiar books and toys with him in this barren place. How would he ever get used to sharing this huge empty room with so many other boys?

"Nicholas, you must exchange your world's clothing for Shaker clothing," Andrew said. "All Shakers are equal and all dress alike."

Nicholas hated to exchange his favorite shirt for the old-fashioned Shaker costume, but, to his amazement, a Shaker brother measured him for three sets of new clothing: a set of work clothes and two suits for Sunday. This was more new clothing than he had ever owned.

Next, Andrew took Nicholas to meet the sister who helped him care for the boys. "Welcome, young Nicholas. I am Lucy, caretaker of your clothing and nurse when you are sick. Every sleeping room in the village is assigned a number. All of your clothing will be marked with the number of the *Boys' House* and your name," she said. "The sisters will pick up the soiled clothing and return it clean to the Boys' House. Nicholas, you will be responsible for keeping your clothing in perfect order in your drawer or on your assigned pegs."

Sister Lucy looked sternly at him, but she had a twinkle in her eye. "Do you understand, Nicholas? Please learn what Mother Ann has taught us about housekeeping. 'Clean your rooms well; for good spirits will not live where there is dirt. There is no dirt in heaven.' "

"Is Mother Ann your mother, Sister Lucy?"

"Nay and yea, child. She is my spiritual mother, not my birth mother. She will be your mother, too, Nicholas. Mother Ann guides all Shakers and sends them gifts of wisdom and love on the wings of her heavenly doves."

At precisely eleven-thirty, a bell rang and the other boys appeared, giving Nicholas his first look at his new companions. Andrew signaled the boys and they lined up in double-file, each according to his age. After Nicholas was placed in line, Andrew marched them in step to the dwelling house. They entered a small room Andrew called the *Brothers' Waiting Room.* All around the room were rows of pegs upon which hung blue-and-white napkins, each marked with a name.

Shaker drawing.

Table Monitor

Here then is the pattern
Which Jesus has set;
And his good example
We cannot forget;
With thanks for his blessings
His word we'll obey;
But on this occasion
We've something to say.

What we deem good order,
We're willing to state,
Eat hearty and decent,
And clear out our plate,
Be thankful to Heaven
For what we receive,
And not make a mixture
Or compound to leave.

We find of those bounties
Which Heaven does give,
That some live to eat,
And that some eat to live-
That some think of nothing
But pleasing the taste,
And care very little
How much they do waste.

"I must explain the dining room rules to you now," Andrew said, "because we are not allowed to talk at the dinner table.

"We *Shaker our plates.* This means food is placed on the plate in an orderly fashion. Don't mix food together or make it look messy. You may help yourself to as much as you like, but you are expected to eat everything you put on your plate. All traces of food are wiped from the plate with pieces of bread and eaten. When you finish eating, watch the other boys and arrange your knife and fork on the plate the same way they do. I will teach you a verse called 'Table Monitor' from our Juvenile Guide of Good Manners.

"Our meal today will be a special treat. The sisters are changing kitchen crews. Brothers and sisters change jobs from time to time so the work will not become dull. Every time the sisters change places in the kitchen we get a special treat. We will surely have cake sweetened with real sugar instead of molasses."

The boys talked quietly while they waited to eat. After what seemed to Nicholas an eternity, a bell rang and they marched in orderly Shaker fashion into the dining hall. The girls were entering the room from an identical doorway on the opposite side. Nicholas saw his sister, Julia, across the room and felt a pang of sadness. He would only see her from a distance now.

He had never been in such a large dining room. There was no covering on the tables, but the wood was beautifully finished. The chairs were the same chairs he saw everywhere in the village, straight-backed with ribbon-woven seats. He counted five long tables, each divided into place settings for four. Andrew called the place settings *squares* and assigned Nicholas to a square with three boys his age.

Before sitting down, everyone knelt in silent prayer. Nicholas prayed that beets would not appear at this meal. It was difficult to concentrate on serious prayer while delicious smells filled the room and he was hungry.

He was surprised to see a blue-and-white-striped quart mug at his place. He had never before been allowed so much milk at one meal. The first food dish was placed by a sister in the center of the square. As the boys emptied the dish, the sister filled it again. Nicholas ate carefully and did his best to "Shaker his plate."

He was relieved when the dessert, generous pieces of the most delicious cake, appeared on the table. There was no way he could accidentally mix cake with other food because there was nothing else on the plate. It was his pleasure to eat every morsel without worrying about keeping it in perfect order.

When the meal was over, Andrew gave a signal and the boys neatly folded their napkins and quietly marched in step from the dining room. They broke into a run as soon as they left the building.

"Come on, Nicholas," a friendly boy named John called out, "Saturday afternoon is our free time. We can work in our gardens down at the Island."

"Two years ago," Andrew said, "the boys helped me clear this land from a wilderness of rocks and bushes. We worked the soil to a soft fineness. Then we made a road connecting it with the land. The garden plots are separated by rows of apple trees. Each boy old enough to use tools has his own plot, and you'll have one, too. Next year you can plant anything you please."

"I would like to grow a garden, Andrew. What will I plant? And what is a mill pond?"

"Slow down, Nicholas. You ask too many questions. Most of the boys grow popcorn, melons, and tomatoes, but you can choose anything you like from our large supply of Shaker garden seeds."

"*Mill ponds* help us work. Water runs downhill through the eight

Tho' Heaven has bless'd us
With plenty of food;
Bread, butter, and honey
And all that is good;
We loathe to see mixtures
Where gentle folk dine,
Which scarcely look fit
For the poultry or swine.

We find often left,
On the same china dish,
Meat, applesauce, pickle,
Brown bread, and minc'd fish;
Another's replenish'd
With butter and cheese;
With pie, cake, and toast,
Perhaps, added to these.

Let none be offended
At what we here say;
We candidly ask you
Is that the best way?
If not, lay such customs
And fashions aside,
And take this monitor
Henceforth for your guide.

Canterbury boys eating apples on Boys' Island.

Canterbury mill ponds. We control the flow of water between ponds with dams and spillways. When we let the water loose it turns *mill* wheels and makes power for us. We use our water wisely. Nicholas, when the Canterbury Shakers are finished with the water it is all worn out."

Only a few days before a boy had left the village, and Andrew gave his garden plot to Nicholas. Nicholas could sense the envy of the other boys.

"This is one of the finest plots on the Island," Andrew said. "If you remember the Shaker motto, 'Hands to Work, Hearts to God,' beauty, love, and joy will grow with your plants. Now, come with me to the third mill pond. I want to show you how the beaver makes his dam."

At three o'clock the boys found their places in the Boys' Shop. Sister Lucy

Beaver dam in Canterbury mill pond.

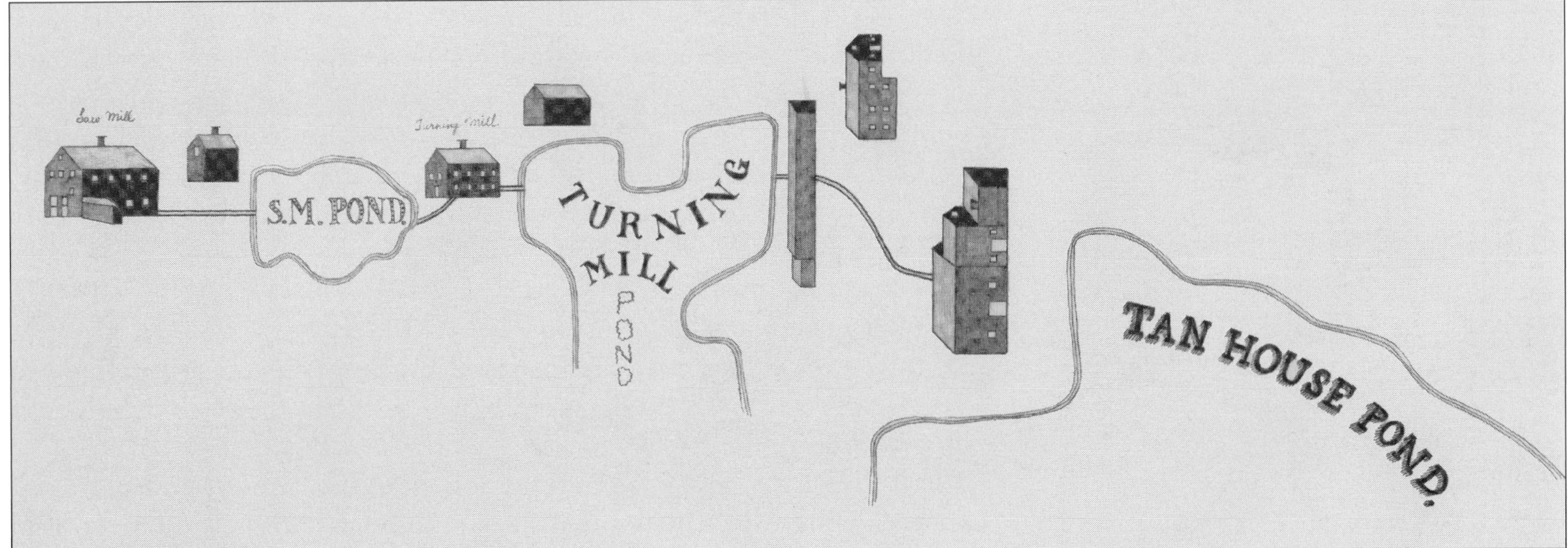

Diagram of Canterbury mill pond system.

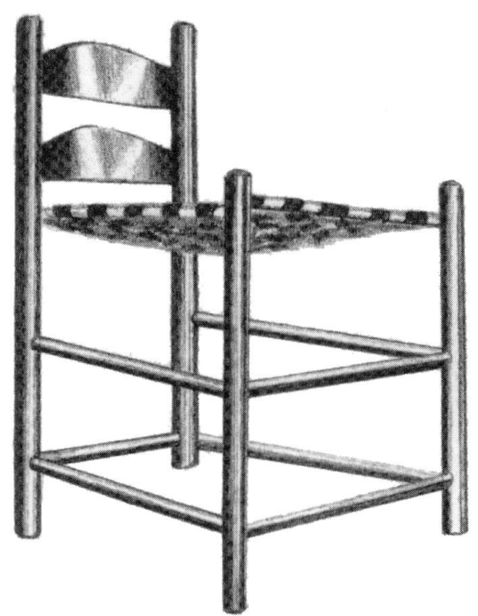

Above: Clock angel from a Shaker drawing.
Below: Shaker chair.

had left a clean bundle of clothing for each one. The boys took the bundles and followed Andrew to a mill pond for a bath.

Well-scrubbed boys returned to the Shop and changed into their second-best Sunday suits. Under Sister Lucy's supervision, the soiled work clothes from the previous week were gathered in a basket and carried to the laundry.

Andrew marched the boys to a large barren room used only on Sunday. Nicholas shivered. There was not even a rug on the floor to add warmth. A large wood stove used for heat in winter stood in the middle. Near it was a long table. There was a row of chairs with the now familiar woven seats, one for each boy, the same as the Boys' Shop.

The boys automatically sat in their assigned places. Andrew disappeared inside a small closet. Beginning with the oldest, each boy visited him in the closet. The others sat silently and waited their turn. This was very hard for the little boys. When it was his turn, Nicholas entered the closet with butterflies in his stomach. He had no idea what would happen inside.

"Before you become a Shaker," Andrew said, "you must confess your world's sins. This is an important part of our religion. Although you are speaking to me, Nicholas, your confession is really made to God and I am only here to witness your honesty. You'll confess your sins today and every Saturday from now on."

Nicholas stammered, "I don't know what to confess."

Gentle Andrew seemed to understand his problem but did nothing to clear it up. After a talk on proper behavior for a Shaker boy, Nicholas was allowed to leave the closet.

At bedtime, the boys knelt in front of their chairs and said a silent prayer. Andrew reminded them all talking was forbidden from this moment until the morning. The boys were required, on this night only, to sleep on their backs, with hands pressed together near their faces as if in prayer. Andrew inspected each bed to make sure the boys were in the proper position. Nicholas fell asleep worrying what would happen if he moved during the night. How would he ever be able to keep all of these rules straight? Perhaps he was not perfect enough to live in the Shaker's heaven on earth.

Nicholas was awakened at four-thirty the next morning by the ringing of the great bell. Some of the boys were dressed before the bell stopped ringing. They knelt in silent prayer for a few minutes and raced out to the cow barn. This was Nicholas's first trip to the gigantic Church Family barn. A grassy ramp led up to the entrance.

"Our barns are the best in the county," Andrew said proudly. "Shakers find ways to save work because Mother Ann taught us 'You must not lose one moment of time, for you have none to spare.' The earthen ramps at either end of the barn make it possible to drive loaded hay wagons in at the hayloft level, unload them, and drive straight out again without turning around. This is much easier than laboring to pitch hay up to the hayloft. We keep our cows on the first floor so we can feed them easily by dropping the hay down at feeding time. And the pit where manure is composted into fertilizer is on the floor below the stalls. It's a very practical barn, yea?

"We heated the barn last winter, Nicholas, and milk production soared. I will give you a very pleasant cow to care for. She will be your responsibility."

After a noon meal of cold boiled rice, baked beans, and apple pie, the boys gathered for *retiring time* to sit for one half-

Drawing of the Canterbury barn that was destroyed by fire.

Shaker sisters preparing a meal.

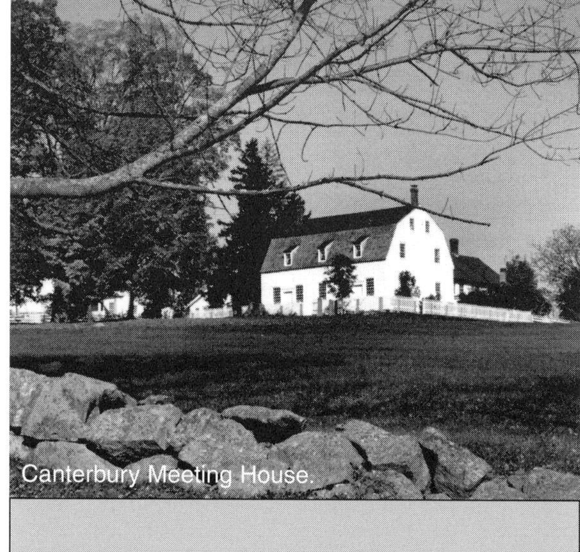

I Will Bow and Be Simple

I will bow and be simple,
I will bow and be free,
I will bow and be humble,
Yea bow like the willow tree.

I will bow, this is the token,
I will wear the easy yoke,
I will bow and be broken, Yea.
I'll fall upon the rock.

hour in solemn silence in preparation for the worship service. Nicholas felt drowsy after the heavy meal and almost fell asleep in his chair.

At one-thirty the entire village gathered outside the Meeting House. Men and boys removed their coats before entering the *Meeting Room.*

"Coats are not worn during Sunday meetings," Andrew said, "because the worship of God demands a zeal and activity of body no less than should at least equal manual labor, and we would not think of wearing a fine coat when we work. Nicholas, I think you have never witnessed a worship service like ours. It consists of considerable physical activity. The singing and dancing are expressive of the zeal, spirit, and love our people feel for God and each other. Only by expressing these strong emotions physically is it possible for us to reach proper spiritual depth.

"The heavenly blue color in our meeting room comes from a special Shaker paint. If I gave you one hundred chances to tell me what makes the paint blue, I know you would never guess the color comes from blueberries and buttermilk.[1]"

Concentrating on keeping in step, Nicholas marched into the meeting room, bowed low, and tiptoed to the west side of the room where he stood in a row with the other boys. Julia and the girls entered in an identical manner from a door across the room and stood in a row facing the boys.

Nicholas looked around the room at the beautiful blue color and wondered how paint could be made from blueberries and buttermilk. If he stayed with the Shakers, he would someday learn to make the blue paint.

His daydream was interrupted by the elders and eldresses entering from opposite sides. They bowed and seated themselves on the north side of the room. A little bell rang and the rest of the families entered, men through one door and women through the other door, all bowing and forming rows,

1. Shaker stories that have been passed down by word-of-mouth claim the paint is made from blueberries and buttermilk. A recent anaylsis shows the paint was actually made with a lead, not a milk, base. It was colored with Prussian blue pigment.

men and women facing each other.The service began with the singing of a Shaker hymn. After a few words of prayer, the head elder said, "We will now go forth in the Square Order," and the families performed a beautiful and precise dance.

Nicholas was used to sitting quietly in church. The Shaker service was entirely different. There was no organ or piano. All hymns were sung by voice alone. Most of the service was made up of energetic movement and dancing, which continued until everyone was tired. He could guess how the Shakers got their name. The energetic dancing could easily be mistaken for shaking.

Supper followed the service. The main dish was a special treat Nicholas had never tasted before, beans prepared with rich cream. It was delicious.

After finishing supper and the milking, the boys returned to the Sunday Room. Moving chairs into a semicircle, each one in turn chose a favorite Shaker hymn for the group to sing. After the singing was over, Nicholas found himself humming "I Will Bow and Be Simple." He would ask Andrew to help him learn the hymn and request it next week.

Monday morning the wake-up bell rang at four o'clock, half an hour earlier than usual, because it was washing day. Nicholas and his new friend John planned to use the extra time to pick berries. Armed with baskets, they headed out to search the woods for berry bushes.

"We'll eat as many berries as we can," John said. "If we pick more than we can eat, we'll trade them with the nurse for candy. She likes to give the sick a special treat of wild berries."

Nicholas longed for candy and vowed silently to pick berries until the season was over.

At the end of his first week in the Boys' House, Andrew took Nicholas for a walk. "Today we'll plant a young tree and name it 'Nicholas.' You must care

Hop Up and Jump Up

Hop up and jump up and whirl
'round, whirl 'round,
Gather love, here it is, all 'round,
all 'round.
Here is love flowing 'round,
Catch it as you whirl 'round.
Reach up and reach down,
Here it is all 'round.

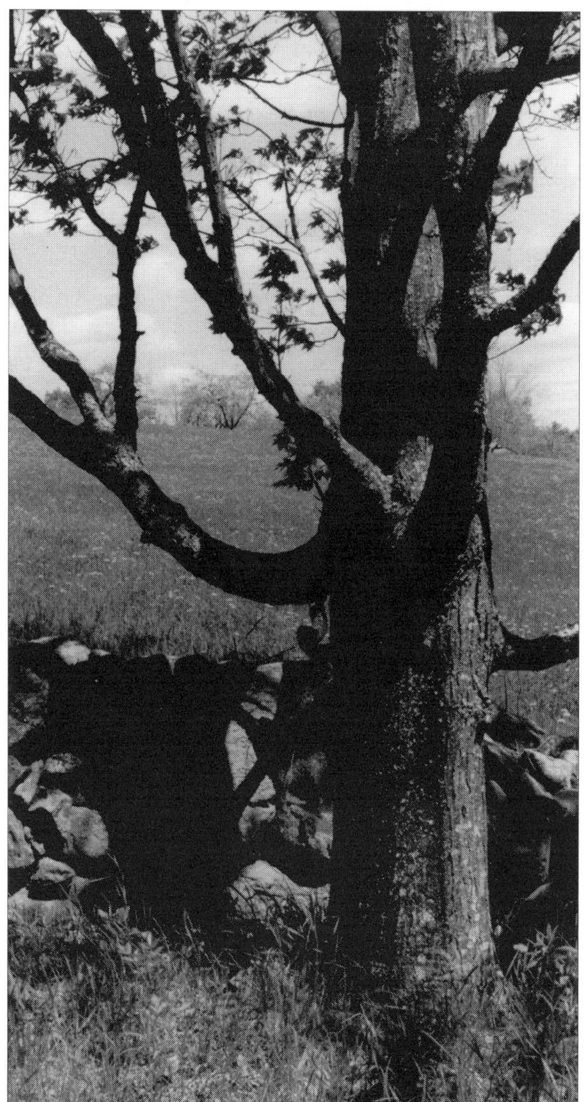

A tree planted long ago by a child at Canterbury.

for this tree and protect it from all harm. Together you will grow roots and become strong members of our community."

Andrew dug a hole near the Meeting House, between the stone wall and the road, and they planted the sapling named Nicholas.

Day by day, Nicholas was adjusting to the Shaker routine. From time to time he talked to his sister Julia at *union meetings.* At these times small groups of men and women, boys and girls, eight or ten of each sex, would spend an hour together in the evening eating popcorn, drinking cider, and talking. Except for the separation from his family, the life was agreeable to him. Andrew was a kind man and he seemed to anticipate when Nicholas was homesick for his mother. Then he was taken to see her, but he was never left alone with her. Andrew or another Shaker was always present in the room with them. However, this was only a small trouble, for his life was busy and he was happy.

Summer view of Canterbury Shaker Village.

Fall 1852

In farm communities fall is synonomous with harvest time, and so it was in the Shaker village at Canterbury, New Hampshire. Great excitement filled the air in the Boys' House, for soon it would be haying time. Nicholas knew nothing about haying but he found himself looking forward to it with eager anticipation. In the city he had started back to school in the fall. In the Shaker village, fall was still a school holiday for the boys. It was a Shaker practice to have boys and girls attend school at different times of the year. This practice kept the children separated and made the boys available when needed to help full-time with the farm work. Since fall harvesting was a busy time for the brothers, the girls attended school and the boys worked.

When the hay was finally ready for cutting, Andrew took the boys to the tool room after breakfast and gave each one a pitchfork. Holding pitchforks to their shoulders like rifles, they marched in Shaker order double-file out of the barnyard. Then they all ran helter-skelter to the hay fields where the brothers, more than thirty of them, were already hard at work cutting hay by hand. The boys' job was spreading the freshly cut hay to dry. It was easy work, and they made a game of it, chasing after each other and then tumbling and rolling in the hay.

Fall days were happy. In the mornings the brothers cut and the boys spread the hay. In the afternoons, Andrew helped the boys rake the hay into small conical piles while the brothers carted the hay cut the day before to a storage barn. Meals were eaten picnic style in the fields, and cold drinks were carried to the workers in a wagon several times a day. Nicholas sampled homemade lemon, peppermint, checkerberry (wintergreen), raspberry, and currant fruit

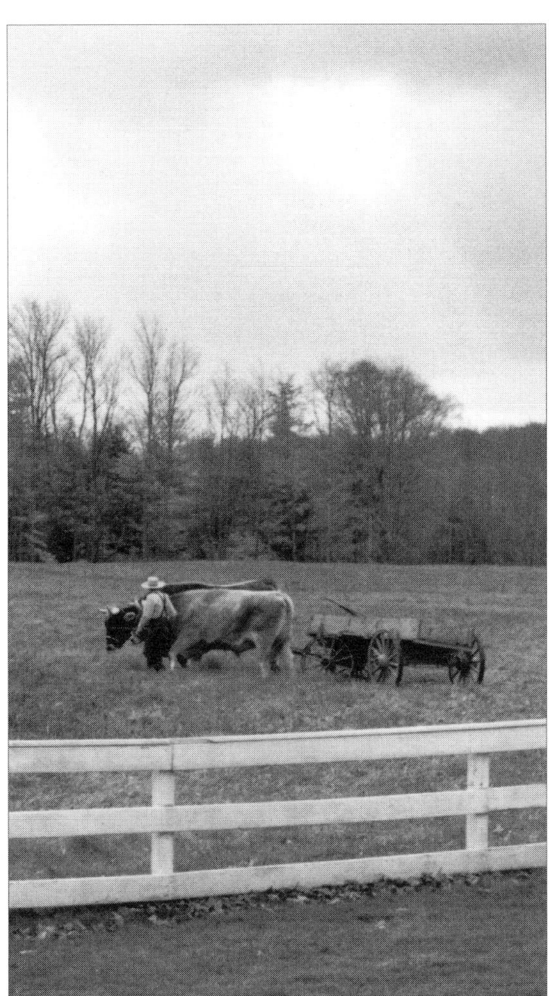

Harvest time in a Shaker village.

Old Canterbury Shaker labels.

drinks and a sweet, fresh buttermilk he liked best of all. Many workers made the work light and the huge fields were cleaned in a few days.

After the haying was finished, the brothers and the boys, harvested crops of oats, barley, beans, corn, potatoes, and apples. The Canterbury Shaker apple orchards were famous for the size of their yield and the excellent quality of their fruit. Most of the family, brothers and sisters, boys and girls, were occupied an entire week harvesting the apple crop. The brothers picked and the sisters sorted and placed the apples in baskets according to size and quality. While the family worked on the apple harvest, dinner was served in an old barn near the orchard. Nicholas was surprised at being allowed to talk while eating in the barn. He enjoyed these meals more than any he had eaten with the Shakers. He longed for the companionship of the dinner conversations he had shared with his real family in Providence. Perhaps, he thought, Shakers are not allowed to talk in the dwelling house dining room because it is so very crowded. If many people are allowed to talk at the same time in a room the noise is deafening.

The baskets of apples were carried in wagons from the barn to the village where the top grades with no blemishes or bruises were carefully transferred to cold storage bins in the cellar. The lower-grade apples were put aside until they could be prepared for drying. Dried apples would be used in the spring to make apple pies, which were a mainstay of the family diet, and they would be made into Shaker applesauce and sold to the world's people.

"Shaker applesauce is like no other," Andrew told Nicholas. "Dried pieces of apple are reconstituted in a lovely rich, thick syrup made from boiling Shaker-made apple cider until the volume is greatly reduced." Nicholas remembered how much he had enjoyed the warm, chunky Shaker applesauce served to him when his family first arrived at the Trustee's Office.

He looked forward to apple-drying evenings. The entire family would gather together in the laundry room to cut and prepare the apples. The pleasant work made time fly by. Everyone forgot the day's weariness and spent the evening hours working together for the common good of the community. It was a cheerful, animated scene. Homemade tallow candles gave the laundry room its only light. The brothers sat on one side of the room and the sisters on the other. With two special machines of Shaker invention, the brothers efficiently peeled and quartered the apples. The sisters, boys, and girls finished the apple quarters for drying in the *kiln.* They sat at long tables, each with a wooden tray. Mary Whitcher watched over them to be sure the work was properly done. This was especially important to her because her job as a trustee was to sell applesauce and other Shaker-made products to the world. Mary's good economic sense helped keep the family prosperous.

Because the boys were taken on a camp-style outing, Nicholas found wood chopping a close second favorite to apple harvesting. With Andrew's help, they carried their dinner to the woods, built a fire, baked potatoes, roasted apples and green corn in the hot ashes, and cooked fresh meat over the fire on the end of a stick. They roasted beechnuts and chestnuts found in the woods for dessert.

Shaker brothers and sisters working together on family products.

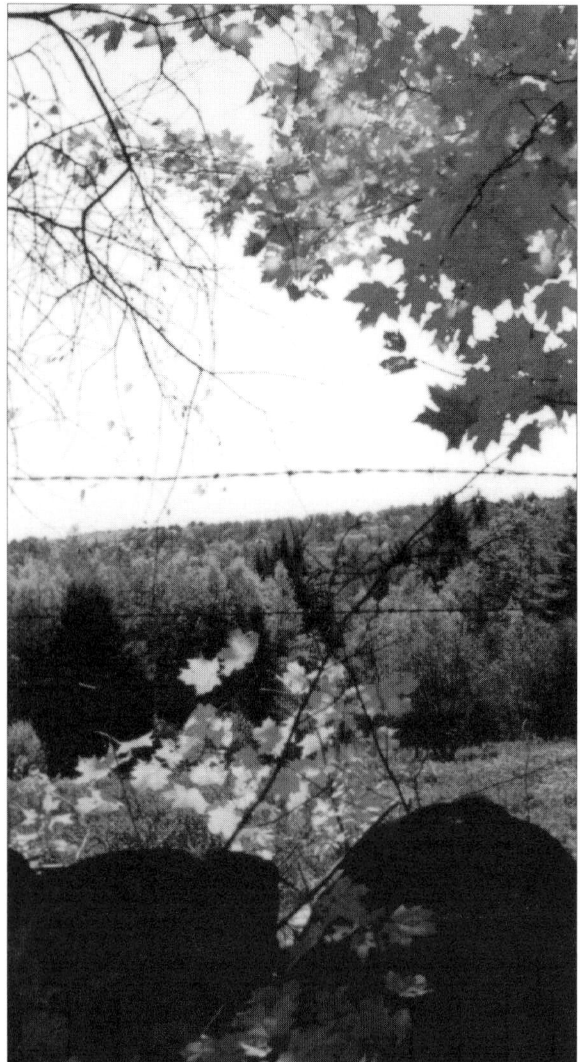

Fall in New Hampshire.

To keep the boys from forgetting their lessons, Andrew devoted one half-day each week to reviewing what had been learned in the previous school term. During the warm fall weather he allowed the boys several half-day holidays from their routine work. On these happy afternoons they would tramp over the pasture land and through the woods sometimes as far as five miles from the village. Or they would stay close to home and play ballgames in a grassy field. Nicholas looked forward to rainy afternoons because Andrew took the boys fishing. He made them wear thick woolen raincoats over their clothes, but they had fun getting wet in spite of the rainproof clothing.

After the harvests were over and the horses could be spared, the children, boys and girls in turn, were treated to a day away from the village. John told Nicholas all about these happy trips. In past years they were driven through a large town to see the sights.

This year a really special trip was planned. The Canterbury boys were to meet with the boys from Chosen Vale, the Shaker village at Enfield, New Hampshire, for a picnic at a midway point, approximately forty-eight miles from each village. They were very excited about this unusual event and they talked of it in eager anticipation. When at last the day of the trip arrived, the Canterbury boys were up before dawn. The weather looked forbidding, but when the sun came up, it turned out to be a fine day. They ate breakfast and set off with Andrew driving the best village wagon.

They reached the meeting place in great spirits, but found no boys from Enfield waiting to greet them. Andrew drove on toward Enfield, but to everyone's great disappointment they did not meet up with the Enfield boys. Sadly they headed back to Canterbury. The boys were terribly disappointed.

In those days there were no telephones, and the nearest telegraph office was eleven miles from the village. When the unhappy boys returned, a kindly

Shaker brother greeted them with news from the telegraph office. It had looked so much like bad weather at Enfield that the caretaker, thinking the weather at Canterbury would be the same, had canceled the trip. Smiling at the dejected boys, Andrew promised they would repeat the trip in one week.

On a crisp, sunny fall morning they set out a second time. This time the boys from Enfield were waiting for them at the midway point with a delicious picnic spread out. The Canterbury boys added to the bountiful spread and they all feasted and exchanged stories of life in their villages.

One Enfield boy described the economic history of his village very well. "Because we are a communal society and pool all of our money together, our founders were able to purchase the best land. A successful Shaker village needs

Below left: Canterbury mill pond.
Below right: Enfield dwelling house.

Old advertisement for Canterbury Dorothy cloak.

fertile land for farming and water for manufacturing. Our village has an abundance of both. Our land surrounds beautiful Mascoma Lake. Because most of our village was once under water, crops grown in our fields are bountiful."

A boy from Canterbury explained that his village had a rougher time of it. The land they acquired was fertile and well situated, but there was no water available for mill power. The brothers dug by hand a water system of eight ponds, connected with spill-ways and dams. This was surely an incredible feat.

Not to be outdone, a boy from Enfield told about the bridge cleverly constructed across Mascoma Lake by the brothers four years ago. One hundred and fifty trees, at least sixty feet in length, were driven into the lake bottom. When the water froze, rafts were constructed on the ice between the log supports. These rafts were filled with heavy stones, and when the ice around the rafts melted, they sank to the bottom of the lake. This process was patiently repeated until a bridge emerged from Mascoma Lake.

"John," whispered Nicholas, "I didn't know Shakers were so competitive."

"We are," answered John, and then he spoke to the group. "Elder Henry Blinn lives with our family. He is surely the most important Shaker alive. He is at the same time a beekeeper, tailor, cabinetmaker, blacksmith, tinsmith, printer, writer, stone cutter, engraver, teacher, and a great orator. Sister Dorothy Durgin has just finished making a cape so beautiful that all the fine ladies of the world will want one. And I'll bet anyone that our sister Mary Whitcher sells the most dried herbs and Shaker applesauce."

Then the Enfield boys boasted of their Great Stone Dwelling House, the largest building north of Boston. One of the younger boys said, "It is a gigantic building, six stories high with twenty-four very large sleeping rooms. It took our brothers five years to make five hundred built-in cupboards and eight hundred built-in drawers."

Gradually talk shifted to news from other villages. The Mount Lebanon community had just published their first furniture catalog featuring distinctive Shaker-style chairs with ribbon-woven seats. The chairs were selling in great quantity and it was a profitable business. The boys from both villages felt great pride in the success of the Shakers' business enterprises.

At last it was time to head home. As they said good-bye, Nicholas promised to write to a boy from Enfield. All returned to the village in high spirits, anxious to share their experience with the other members of the family.

After the first frost when the chestnut trees were full of ripe nuts, Nicholas and John found time to run out to a grove half a mile away from the village to gather nuts. By now Nicholas had learned that it was the village custom to share half of the harvest with the old people in the village. But he did not mind because he had learned that there was always a candy reward for gifts to the elderly.

"Andrew is very kind," John said. "Last winter he gave us many special treats. If we give our nuts to him, I know he will sell them and buy us a surprise."

Nicholas longed for surprises because they made him feel like he was living with his family again. But Andrew's kind indulgences were soon to end, for in the late fall he was replaced by Joseph. This was a great blow for Nicholas, who had grown very fond of Andrew. Joseph, the new caretaker, was very strict and seemed to favor some boys over the others. Life was not as happy with Joseph as it had been with Andrew. Fortunately, Nicholas had been raised by his own loving parents who taught him good manners and cheerful obedience. He was therefore one of the boys most favored by Joseph.

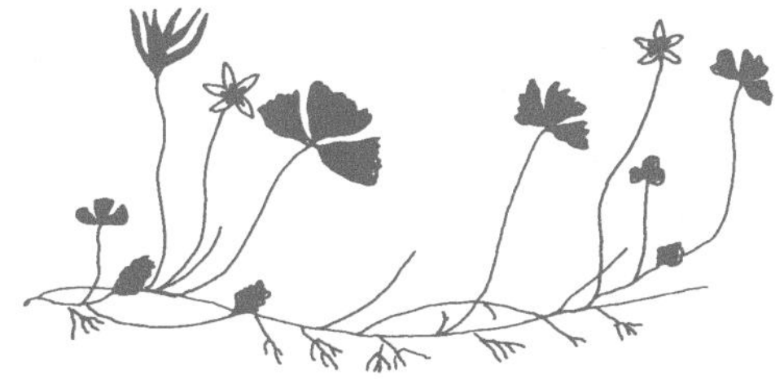

Shaker-made rocker.

A Shaker brother carrying maple sugar buckets.

Winter 1853

New Hampshire wintertime weather is cold, dull, and dreary. Nicholas missed the excitement of the Christmas season. To his disappointment, the Shakers' only observance of Christmas was a solemn service in the Meeting House. He found himself longing for any change in the dull daily routine of his life. To make matters worse, it was his turn to attend school. He was bored and missed his own family and Andrew. Even the occasional opportunity to talk to his sister at the weekly union meetings did little to cheer him up. Time passed uneventfully until after school closed the last week in February. Then an event occurred that shattered the entire community.

Three of the young brothers, one of them the schoolteacher, disappeared one day. When they did not return by sundown, it was obvious to everyone in the family that the three men had left to live in the world. Because they had lived with the Shakers since early childhood, leaving without a word of good-bye was unimaginable.

One by one everyone, even Nicholas, was questioned about the disappearance. If anything was learned, the information was never shared with the boys. This tragic event made Nicholas painfully aware that leaving the community to live in the world was a shameful event.

John explained to Nicholas that the three young brothers had vanished without a word intentionally. Any Shaker who spoke of a desire to leave the community was called into the elder's office and submitted to intense pressure from other family members. No effort was spared to persuade the unhappy Shaker to stay.

Nicholas thought how strongly these men must have longed to see the

The maple grove and camp were located about 2 miles from the Canterbury Shaker Village. The sugar season began the first of March and usually closed on April 10.

world for them to leave their safe home and their loved ones.

The memory of this tragic event was lessened by the arrival of maple sugar season. The boys happily helped the brothers in the pleasant task of harvesting the maple syrup at a camp set up about two miles from the village in an orchard of exceptionally large and productive maple trees.

Bundled up in their warmest winter clothing, the boys first drove spigots into holes in the trees. Later in the morning,

Shaker brothers tapping a maple tree. The Canterbury trees were tapped every year for more than forty years.

a few sisters came down to the camp and helped the boys to scald the sugar buckets. Then they tramped through deep snow distributing the clean buckets among the spigoted trees. Before the sisters left, they cooked pancakes and served them with a jug of the best syrup from the previous year.

The happy days spent at the maple sugar camp reminded Nicholas of harvest time in the fall. The boys played in the snow and ate unlimited amounts of candy made from the fresh maple syrup. Nicholas never dreamed there could be so many different kinds of candy made from one ingredient.

First John and Nicholas opened the syrup can and tasted the sweet contents. Then they made "stick chops" by boiling the maple sugar down to a very thick mass and pouring it on the snow to harden. When Nicholas warmed a stick chop in his mouth it became elastic, almost like a piece of taffy. Next, he watched an older boy pour boiled syrup on a marble slab and knead it into a white candy that had a very different taste from the stick chop. Last, he helped place a large bucket filled with raw sap outside the camp building to freeze. When it was finally hard to the touch, the frozen contents were cracked open to expose a small amount of thick, clear syrup, called "sap honey." Sap honey, Nicholas discovered, had quite a different flavor from ordinary maple syrup. John told him that sugar made from sap honey was white rather than brown.

While the maple sap flowed rapidly, the brothers each took a turn staying all night at the camp to tend the kettles. When it was Joseph's turn, he took Nicholas with him. Nicholas had a great time sitting up most of the night tending the fires and the syrup. He could hear woodland sounds — sounds that were hard to hear in the village — the peeping of the frogs in the little pond near the camp and the hooting of owls in the nearby forest.[2]

2. In rare weather conditions, frogs *can* be out at maple syrup time.

Spring 1853

Spring found Nicholas longing for warmer weather and a chance to be outdoors again. He was happy to return to the maple sugar camp to help the brothers cut firewood, the only source of heat in the village. Big trees were cut from the surrounding forests and hauled to the camp, where the limbs were removed and sawed up using a steam-driven power saw. Men and boys working together, they split the wood into smaller pieces and piled it in sheds to dry over the summer. Then the entire family, including the sisters and girls, formed a working bee and cleaned the camp.

When warmer weather arrived and the frozen earth thawed, Joseph was assigned the care of the kitchen gardens. Nicholas was anxious to help him, for Joseph was a fine gardener and an excellent teacher. Noticing that Nicholas had a special interest in gardening, Joseph placed several areas of the garden in his care: the asparagus bed, a thirty-by-fifty-foot plot of seed being tested for the U.S. government, and a medicinal herb bed of catnip and motherwort. Nicholas had an easy time finding catnip plants in the fields around the village, but motherwort was scarce. He hunted all over the farm and found only enough plants to fill two rows.

As the motherwort grew, Nicholas was horrified to discover that he had mistaken thistle plants for motherwort. He took quite a lot of teasing about his mistake. Even so, he was delighted to have his gardening job because it gave him an opportunity to get away from the other boys who were assigned to size broom corn at the mill. Sometimes he liked to be alone.

Nicholas was not prepared for spring cleaning Shaker style. One morning several sisters walked through every room of the dwelling house singing

Illustration of corn from a Shaker seed packet.

"Sweep sweep and cleanse your floor, Mother's standing at the door" as they made broad sweeping motions with their arms. Joseph said they were following Mother Ann's direction and sweeping clean "the floor of the heart" to keep the family as spotlessly clean spiritually as they were physically.

Preoccupation with the garden helped the time to fly by and soon it was summer again. Nicholas had lived one year with the Shakers. He should have been happy. He had never received an unkind word from Andrew, Joseph, his schoolteacher, or anyone else for that matter, and he had surely been more favored than most of the boys. His life had been pleasant and he had more than enough to eat, but he was not content. Nor was he to be content for the remaining forty-two years he lived with the Canterbury Shakers. He loved his Shaker family, but he never stopped longing for the home he had known with his parents, sister, and brother in Providence, Rhode Island.

Photograph of the Canterbury garden. Notice the boy with a drum.

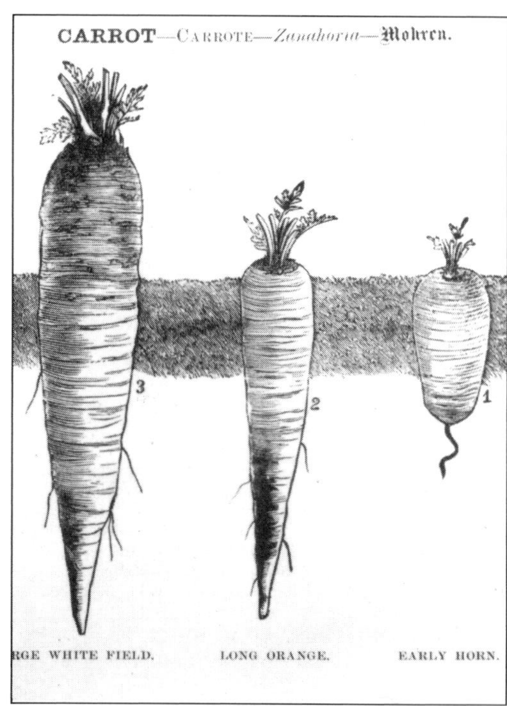

Drawing from a Shaker seed packet.

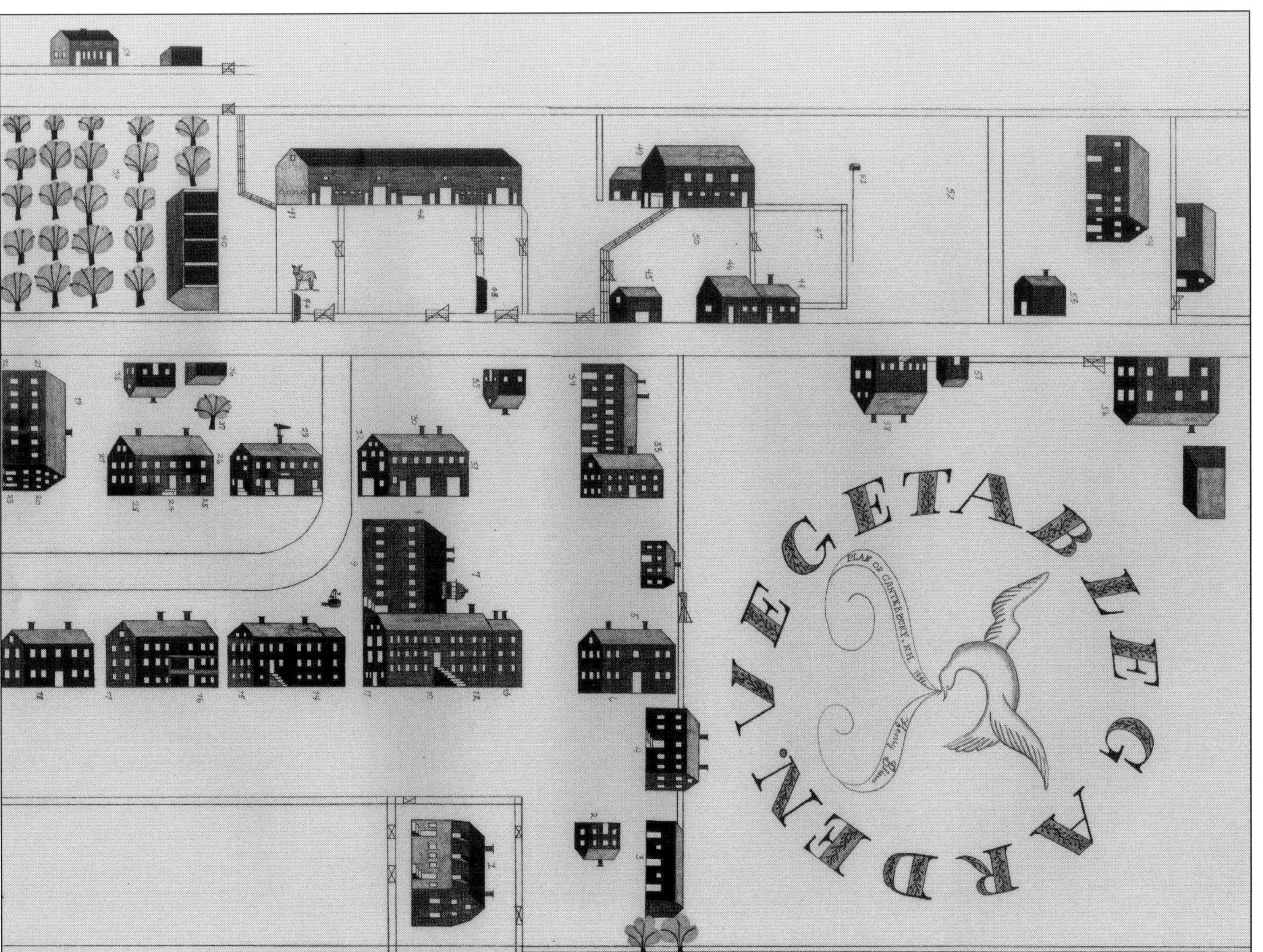

Drawing of Canterbury Shaker Village in the style of Elder Henry Blinn.

Anna Delcheff modeling the Shakers' Dorothy cloak.

Anita Potter

Shaker Girl in 1925

Twelve-year-old Anita Potter sat with Anna Delcheff on the front porch steps. Anna had been her Shaker *caretaker* for over three years until six months ago, when Anna left the Shaker village to live in the world. Anita had been sure she would never see Anna again. Now an unbelievable event had brought them together again. Anita pinched herself to make sure she was not dreaming.

Sadly she remembered back those three years to why she was taken to live with the Shakers. Her Papa was a white-faced, juggling clown who earned his living traveling around the country with the Ringling Brothers circus. After Mama died, he was unable to care for her. The circus was no place for a motherless eight-year-old girl.

A sympathetic friend suggested that Anita be taken to Hancock Shaker Village to be cared for by the kindly Shaker sisters.

"You will be able to visit Anita when you have time away from the circus," the friend said. "And I know she will be well cared for. My daughter is a Shaker sister."

When Papa gently talked about taking her to live in a country village with people called Shakers, Anita felt small and lonely. How could Papa leave her with strangers? But when they arrived at Hancock village and met a little girl named Lillian exactly her same age and another one named Frances a little older, Anita felt much better.

The Shaker sisters told Papa they would be pleased to care for Anita and he was not expected to pay them anything. Anita would, they said, contribute to the work of the village and pay her own way. Papa kissed Anita good-bye and her life as a Shaker girl began.

At Hancock everything was different. Anita now lived with a family of more than twenty-five people. Home was a large dairy farm and her house a huge brick building called a *dwelling house.* There was only one man, Ritcho, and he was called a *brother*. The women were called *sisters* and they all looked the same. It took her a long time to get their names straight, except for the one she liked the best, Anna Delcheff, who was to be her caretaker.

Anna called Anita's new bedroom a *retiring room.* It looked funny to her, especially the bed — a large white iron crib.

"Anna, look," Anita said, "I am too big for this bed. My feet stick out over the end."

"*Yea*, child. We have, at times, sold our furniture when money was needed for our family. I'm sorry, but this is the only extra bed we have now. It will do until we find a bigger one. Help me hang your dresses in the closet. My, this is a pretty coat."

"Mama bought it for me," Anita said proudly.

Anna helped Anita put her favorite doll and her other toys in the neat rows of Shaker drawers. After the long day spent traveling across Massachusetts, Anita was tired.

"Will I sleep alone in this room?" she asked Anna. "This is a very big house."

"*Nay*. Shakers share their retiring rooms. I will sleep here, too."

Together they recited a Psalm from the Bible. Then Anna tucked Anita in

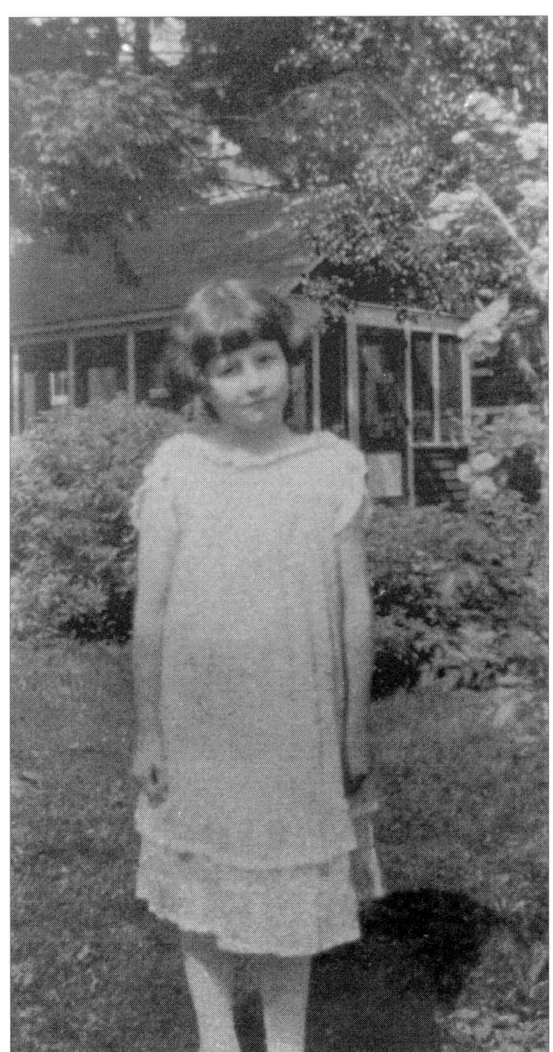

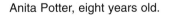

Anita Potter, eight years old.

View of Hancock Shaker Village taken around 1930.

with a big hug. Even though she was in a strange big place and a strange small bed, Anita felt warm and safe.

When she woke up, Anna was still asleep. It was still dark outside, but Anita just couldn't sleep. When Anna was awakened by the five o'clock bell, she found Anita playing house in a tent she made by hanging her quilt over the high sides of the crib.

"Good morning, Anita," Anna said. "How clever you are. It's time to get up. Breakfast is at six o'clock, and it's my job to serve and clean up afterward. You'll help me with my work."

So, on her first morning in the village, Anita learned how to prepare the big Shaker tables for breakfast.

"Because I am your caretaker, it is my duty," Anna said, "to teach you our ideals of *simplicity, order, perfection, cleanliness, health,* and *thrift.* By following these principles every minute of every day, we save time and find ourselves closer to living a *perfect life.* Even though Shakers grow smaller in number every year, our ideals and work will last and the world's people will remember and respect us. Anita, look at the beautiful things our past family members have left for us."

Anna proudly showed Anita the Shaker dining room chairs that fit under the tables, keeping the room looking simple and clean. Anita admired the chair seats, each one woven in different colors.

"Shaker perfection is also beauty," Anna explained. "Our cabinets and chests of drawers are built right into the walls to save space and make our rooms easier to clean. We have pegs around our rooms for hanging chairs out of the way so it is easier to sweep the floor. And when chairs are hanging upside-down, the seats can gather no dust.

"Our village has been here since 1790," Anna continued. "One hundred

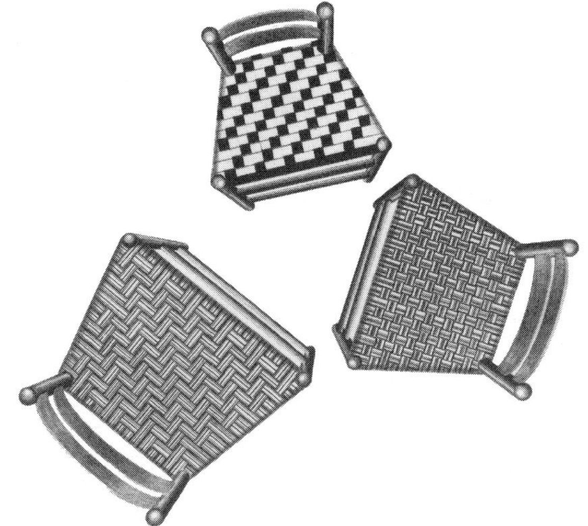

Shaker chair seats woven with chair tape.

Four Hancock Shaker sisters, 1925.

years ago there were many Shaker brothers and sisters living at Hancock. Sometimes our family cared for more than fifty children at one time. Can you imagine one caretaker instructing as many as twenty-five boys or girls? Now we are almost all sisters, and most of the sisters are old."

"Anna, where did the Shakers come from, and where did all the people who used to live here go?"

"The first Shakers came from a dirty city in far-away England. They came to this country with their leader, Mother Ann Lee, looking for religious freedom and a better place to live. When Mother Ann was a girl your age children had to work many hours a day in a factory. It was very unhealthy, and many children died. Mother Ann wanted cleanliness and health for her followers so she directed them to settle in the country on farms and make themselves independent from the rest of the world.

"The Shakers followed her instructions and grew all of their food. And they made everything else they needed — buildings, tools, shoes, clothing — everything you see here. Soon some Shaker villages made special products that other villages didn't have, and they traded. When the villages had more than they could use or trade, they sold to the world's people. Shakers made money selling to the world and their products soon had a reputation for excellent quality. Our seeds, brooms, baskets, chairs, applesauce, and herbal medicines grew into profitable businesses. But as the years passed, some Shakers became unhappy with village life. Many men and women left. The villages became smaller and smaller."

Anna became silent for a time and Anita knew not to ask any more questions. She quietly helped Anna prepare for the family's breakfast, admiring the shape of the little green pitchers as she filled them with thick cream from the Shakers' own dairy cows.

Today, as if to welcome Anita to the village, they were having her favorite breakfast, pancakes served with hot maple syrup. Two dumbwaiters usually carried the food from the downstairs kitchen, but Anna thought them too slow for hot pancakes. So Anita scurried up and down the stairs carrying plates of piping hot pancakes. After breakfast was over, she helped Anna clear the tables, wash the dishes, and set the table in *squares* for the noon meal. After they swept the big dwelling house hallway, Anita was ready for her first day of Shaker school. She had just finished more work than she had ever done in one day and it was only eight o'clock in the morning!

It was winter and very cold, too cold to use the schoolhouse. Teacher Lizzie Belden taught on the third floor of the dwelling house. Six girls attended, three of high school age, Frances in the fifth grade, and Anita and Lillian in the third grade. The schoolroom was heated with a very efficient wood-burning stove. When Anita worked at the blackboard she had to stand in front of the stove, and it burned the back of her legs. Lizzie was not very sympathetic, and from that day on Anita hated working at the blackboard. Just the same, it was an exciting school because all of the grades were together in

Students pose for a group picture in a Shaker classroom, Mt. Lebanon, New York.

Hancock family group portrait, 1925. Anna Delcheff is 1, Anita Potter is 18, and Lillian White is 20.

the same room. When Anita was tired of her own lessons she leaned over and looked at what the older girls were doing.

After school was over, Anita was anxious for a chance to play, but Lillian told her they had to work on their projects first.

"I don't have a project," said Anita.

"Anna will give you one," answered Lillian. "Everyone in our family works hard. We find joy in work and in everything we do."

Anna taught her to knit, and Anita didn't like it at all. The needles were small and made out of steel and the yarn a horrid pink color. Patiently Anna showed her again and again how to make the stitches. Anita tried her hardest to make them just the way Anna did, but Anna was never pleased. She pulled the stitches out again and again. Finally the two girls were given permission to play.

"In the old days," Lillian said, "Shakers were forbidden to keep pets. But, lucky for us, that's changed. My favorite pet is a yellow cat named Theodore Roosevelt Chickenhouse. He has a brother named Billy Chickenhouse. Can you believe that the last cat brothers, named Rufus and Raftus, both lived to be twenty-four years old?"

Anita loved cats and ran off after Lillian to find Theodore Roosevelt Chickenhouse and Billy Chickenhouse.

After supper, Anita helped Anna wash the dishes and set the table for breakfast. "Anna, my mother always put a tablecloth on our kitchen table," said Anita.

"Mother Ann taught us to keep our tables clean enough to eat without cloths," answered Anna. "If we work quickly, Anita, we will have more free time to enjoy this evening."

In the evenings, the sisters gathered in the music room to do handwork and listen to the radio. Anita watched the old sisters knit as fast as lightning. She silently vowed to do the same.

Shaker dog Dewey at the piano.

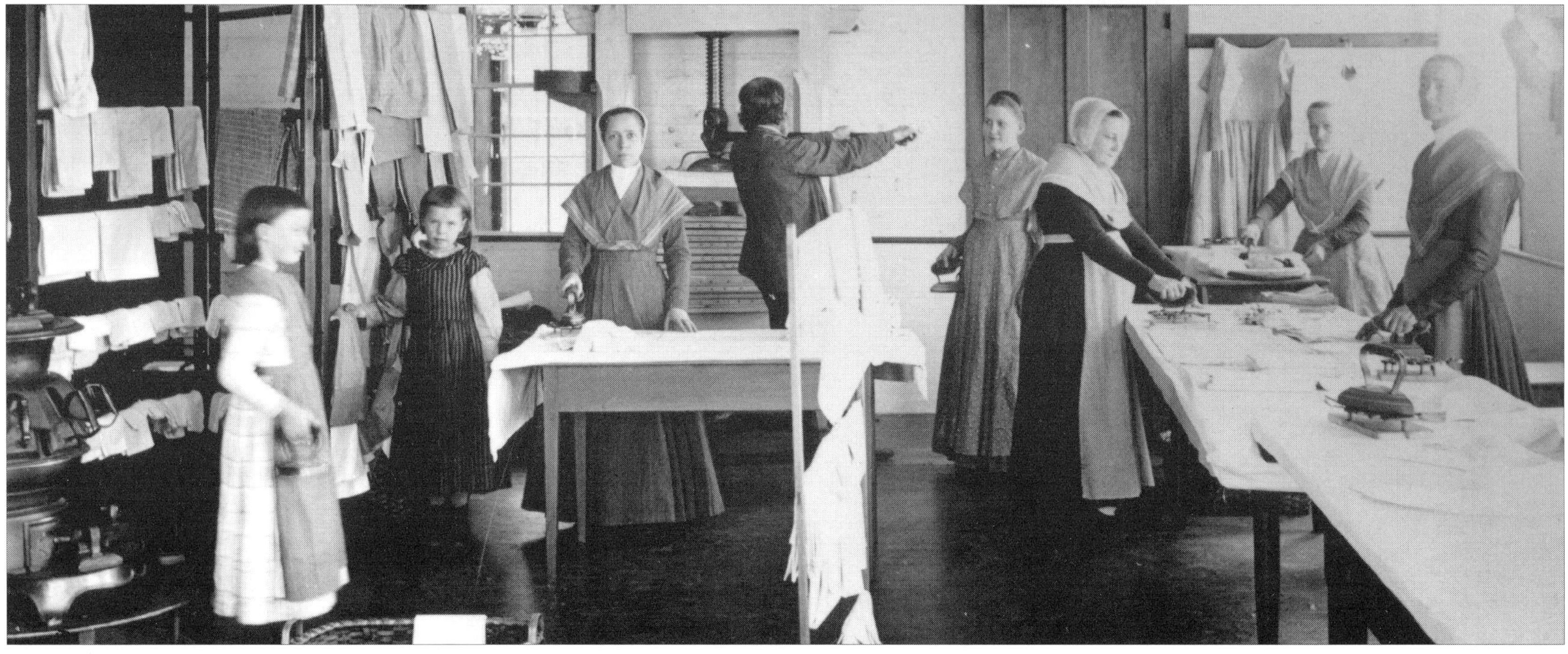

It was a big family, and as Anita got to know them she felt happier. But it was still very hard for her to call the grown-ups by their first names because her Mama had taught her to be respectful. She was happy with her new friends Lillian and Frances. We are, she thought, just like Anna and her friends, sisters Catherine and Jennie. Two of us are exactly the same age, and one a little older.

The rest of the week passed quickly, every day falling into a routine, until Sunday came around. Early Sunday morning everyone lined up outside the Meeting Room and marched in. Sister Jennie played the organ and they sang Shaker hymns. A few sisters stood up and gave testimony. Lillian whispered, "You know, no one dances anymore."

Anita, Lillian, and Frances attended Sunday school in the afternoon, and then spent the rest of the day coloring greeting cards, reading, and going for a walk. On Sunday they had to speak quietly and they were not allowed to play with toys, run, or jump rope.

On Monday, before school, the girls helped the sisters do the laundry. Anita didn't like it because she skinned her knuckles scrubbing handkerchiefs on the rough metal surface of the washboard. Tuesday morning they had to iron the clean handkerchiefs. Anita was taught to take a heavy flat iron from the hot wood-burning stove and press as many handkerchiefs as she could before the iron cooled off. Then she put the cool iron back on top of the stove to warm up and took a hot one. It was hard work and Anita worried about burning herself with an iron.

When the ironing was finished, the three girls, Frances, Lillian, and Anita, delivered a basket of clean clothes to each retiring room in the dwelling house. They ran up and down the long halls with the baskets, determined to finish before it was time for school. According to Lillian and Frances, the best part of the job was delivering a basket to *Eldress* Caroline's room. It was, they promised, exciting, even scary.

"We'll all go together," said Lillian.

"Be careful," said Frances, "she's ancient — over ninety."

The three little girls scurried down the hall, each holding onto the last basket. Giggling, they stopped in front of Eldress Caroline's door and knocked. Slowly the door opened and a wrinkled old face peered out at them. "Yea?"

"Here is your laundry, Eldress Caroline."

"Please put it down over here," she said sternly. "Thank you for carrying it to me." And she glared at each little girl as she pressed a piece of candy into her hand. "Nay, don't run in the hall, dearies!"

Before Anita knew it, one week had passed and she had been too busy to remember to be homesick.

When Anna had time, she taught Anita to sew. "All of the sisters make their own dresses, and you will be no exception," Anna said.

Above: Side view of Hancock dwelling house where Anita Potter lived.
Left hand page: Shaker girls helping sisters iron clothes.

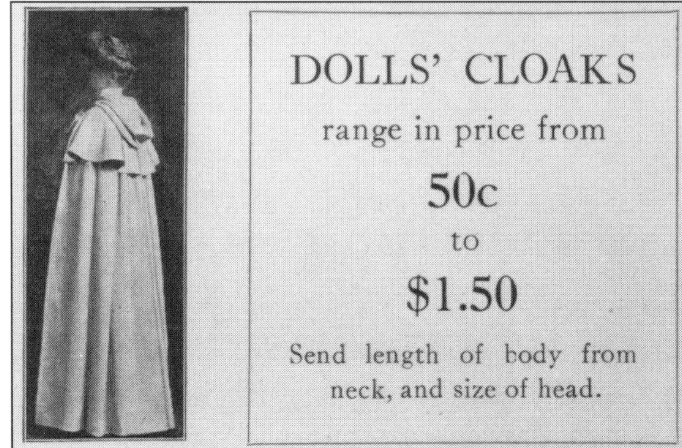

Old Shaker advertisements.

She helped Anita work on a dress of gingham fabric, teaching her to sew the seams by hand, making each stitch perfect and as small as possible. Anita tried her hardest to sew like the sisters who hemmed handkerchiefs with stitches so small it was impossible to see them.

Every day Anita had to complete a sewing or knitting *stint* after school before she was allowed out to play. She learned to work quickly and skillfully, because time saved was hers to spend playing outdoors.

The sisters spent the long winter evenings making *fancywork.* Anita loved to watch old Sister Tilly make tiny acorn *needle emeries.* If she squinted they looked like real acorns. The bottoms were made from soft velvet, but the tops were real acorn caps. Most of the time, Anita worked on the warm scarf she was knitting for her Papa. One evening Sister Catherine, who made flower-covered needle cases, taught Anita how to cross-stitch her name in fancy blue letters.

Ritcho, the only brother, stayed on the brothers' side of the dwelling house. Sometimes in the evenings, instead of going to the music room, a few sisters would go over and visit with him. Anita loved to be invited along because Ritcho had a real *Victrola* in his room, and she could knit and listen to one of his three records.

When the weather warmed up, Anita helped pack the fancywork in two large trunks. She contributed a pair of baby booties she had knit all by herself. Then Anna and sister Jennie dressed in their best clothes and took the trunks to a big expensive hotel in New York state where everything sold in a short time, even the booties. Anita was very proud to have helped earn the family living.

Just after the snow melted, Papa came to visit. They walked together up the reservoir road and found snow-white trailing arbutus peeking through

Modern-day view of the Hancock round barn and vegetable garden.

Shaker cat Theodore Roosevelt Chickenhouse wearing the doll's best clothes.

some decaying leaves near a rocky ledge. It was a happy time. When Papa left, he gave Anita, Lillian, and Frances some money to spend on candy at a store up the road.

On warm, sunny days, the girls would walk up the reservoir road into the woods to search for wildflowers. Anita found her favorite, Dutchman's-breeches, growing in a hidden patch. Then she found Indian pipes and pink lady's slippers. She carefully carried them home to Anna, who showed her how to dry them.

"If you collect enough wildflowers," Anna said, "you can enter them in the Hancock Fair next fall."

Sometimes the three girls would play in their secret hiding place, the circle of old lilac bushes that grew near the dwelling house. Inside the leafy bushes, they sat on old orange crates and had tea parties with their dolls. The Chickenhouse brothers liked to join in the fun for a little cream on a saucer. As their reward the girls let them wear some of the dolls' best clothes.

Now there were two sitting on the brothers' side of the dining room. Richardo had joined Ritcho. Ritcho was in charge of the garden and Richardo took over the job of chauffeur from a hired man. This was an important job, for when the sisters went to town they traveled in style. Brother Richardo drove them in a brand-new, very expensive pale blue Reo automobile. Shakers always felt they were better than the world's people, and it was hard for the three girls not to feel the same way when they were driven in an expensive automobile.

When the warm, lazy days of summer came to western Massachusetts, everyone took time off from work to enjoy the weather — everyone except the Shakers. Anna, Jennie, and Catherine worked harder than ever, cooking, cleaning, washing, ironing, sewing, gardening, canning, raising chickens, selling eggs, and making butter and cheese to sell at the Hancock market.

School was out for a time and the girls helped the sister replace the tape on the dining room chairs that had worn out seats. It was great fun weaving with the colorful handwoven chair tapes.

Busy as they were, Anna and her friends found time to take the girls berry picking on Lebanon Mountain. Anita was sure she could never pick as fast as the skilled sisters. But Anna called her a "good picker" because she filled her pail only with the best berries, free of stems and leaves.

One lucky day when she was off by herself, Anita found a large patch of sweet wild strawberries growing in a hayfield near the reservoir. First she ate as many as she could, and then she brought the rest back to the family. That wonderful day, the sister cooks had enough berries to make delicious strawberry shortcake for the whole family.

When chilly fall weather arrived, an exciting event happened in the dwelling house and Anita slept right through it. The fireman came from the town to extinguish a fire in the chimney of sister Tilly's stove.

The sewing room was taken over by a new project. Anna, Catherine, and Jennie were making the famous Shaker Dorothy opera cloaks to sell to fashionable ladies of the world. Anita especially loved a bright red cloak that hung as a sample on a dressmaker's model.

"Mrs. Grover Cleveland wore a grey Shaker opera cloak to the President's inauguration," Anna said with pride.

In October it was finally time for the Hancock Fair. Everyone from all around the countryside attended. Adults proudly showed off their handcrafts. Children exhibited samples of map making, drawing, penmanship, sewing,

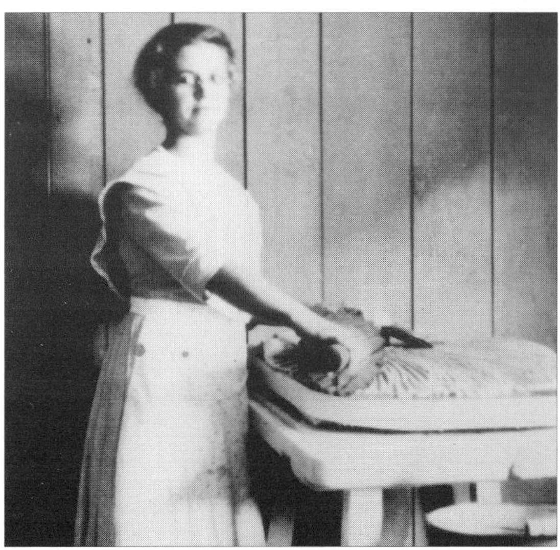

Above: Sister Jennie feeding the chickens.
Below: Sister Catherine making butter.

Hancock Halloween witches' den.

knitting, and collecting, and they even had a spelling bee. Anita won third place in the spelling bee, but she was disappointed that her wildflower entry did not win a prize. She vowed to try harder next year.

The end of the month meant a special party held in the kitchen, sometimes known as the Witches' Den. During the weeks before Halloween, the family worked together in the evenings to make decorations for the party and the sisters whispered about special spooky foods. After school, the Dorothy cloaks were cleared from the big tables in the sewing room so the girls could work on their costumes. Anita's favorite was a spotted clown suit that reminded her of sitting in a big circus tent watching her father perform. The youngest sister, Olive Hayden, was very secretive about her costume. She worked on it when no one else was around. And Olive was missing when the party started. But the girls were so excited they didn't notice until a frightening creature with a coal-black face flew into the Witches' Den on a broom.

The sisters gave Anita, Lillian, and Frances a Thanksgiving project. They were to make table decorations and placecards for every guest at the festive table. After that the girls helped plan the Christmas entertainment, a play the sisters wrote every year. Each of the girls had a part to learn by heart.

Anita was worried about Santa Claus. "How will Santa Claus find me this year?" she asked Anna.

"Don't worry, child," Anna said. "Santa visits our village every year and leaves presents at the foot of every child's bed."

It was indeed a special Christmas, for Papa sent Anna an incredible amount of money, twenty dollars, to buy Anita's Christmas presents. It was too much money. Anna had a hard time spending all of it.

Then came February and Anita's ninth birthday. Sister Olive baked a lovely cake flavored with fragrant Shaker rose water. She called it Mother Ann's

Above: Christmas in the Canterbury dining room.
Below: Shaker music room, Christmas, 1916.

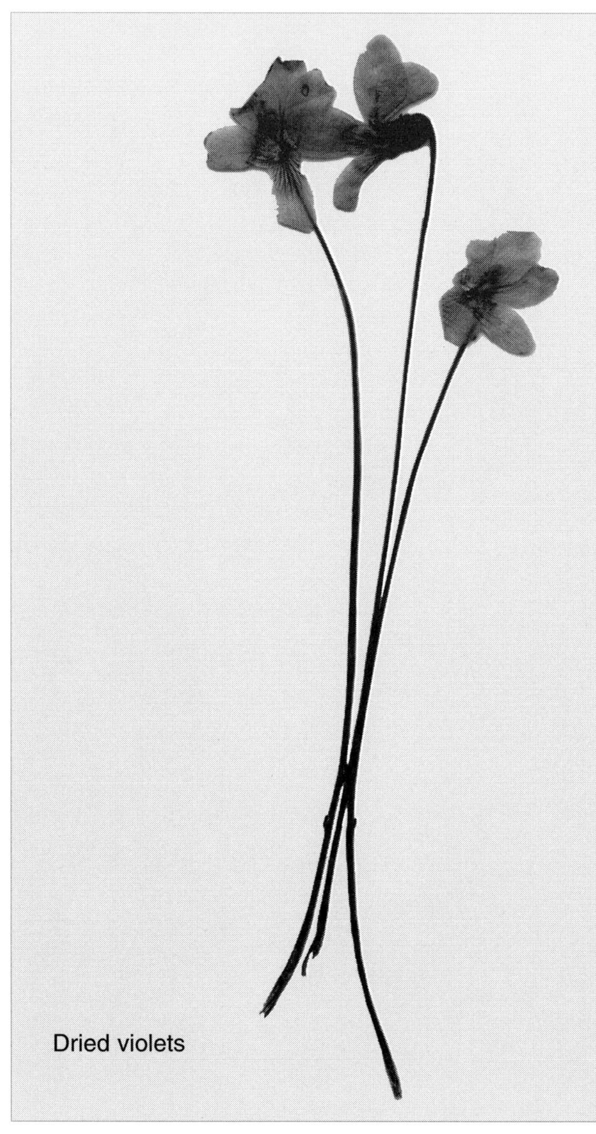
Dried violets

birthday cake. After supper when the family finished feasting on a special meal, Anita opened her presents. There was a book, a hand-painted bookmark, a bar of rose water and glycerin soap, and other small things that made her smile and remember that she was still a little girl apart from the family.

Anita grew used to working hard and time passed quickly. One morning she woke up and realized she had been living at Hancock for more than three years. It was a happy time, especially when she won the spelling bee at the Hancock Fair competing against high school students. Papa visited and she told him the news. He was so proud. "Just think," he boasted, "my daughter can spell better than any youngster in the county."

Next year he was even prouder when she won first prize for her wildflower collection. Anita had, with Anna's help, collected, dried, mounted, and identified 204 different flowers.

She was happy with life in the Shaker village except she knew Anna was not happy. Anna never said so, but Anita could tell something was bothering her. Perhaps it was because Catherine left to work as a nurse. Or because sister Jennie left to marry Mr. White. Anita concentrated on her knitting and Theodore Roosevelt Chickenhouse and the wildflowers growing along the reservoir road. She tried hard not to think about how unhappy Anna was. Then a terrible thing happened.

Anna left the village. Hancock was not the same without her. Anita loved the other family members, but for the first time in her four years at the village, she was unhappy — but not for long. Papa surprised her. He came and took her home to Nowank, Connecticut. There, in an apartment he had just rented, was Anna. And, best of all, she was married to Papa!

Now Anna joined Anita on the porch and they sat sipping lemonade from tall glasses.

"Mmm, Shaker lemonade is good. Anna, why did you leave the Shaker village?"

"Jennie, Catherine, and I were doing most of the work and it was too hard for us. We made butter and cheese to sell at the Hancock market. We took care of the chickens, worked in the garden, cooked for the family, cleaned the dwelling house, did the washing, ironing and sewing, and we made the fancywork. Sometimes we felt we worked without ever stopping. So, we left, one by one, to live in the world where life would be easier."

"Anna," Anita answered, "of all the sisters in the village I was closest to you. When you left, I felt small and alone just like I did when my real mother died. How happy I am to have you here with Papa and me."

Anna

Anita

Activities

The Shakers, past and present, are industrious people who enjoy working with their hands and try always to make objects that are perfect and useful. Fine examples of Shaker perfection in wood, cloth, baskets, metal, and fancywork may be found in many museums. We use well-known Shaker inventions — the flat broom, clothespin, circular saw, and water-powered washing machine — in our daily lives. And Gail Borden was so inspired by the Shaker vacuum pan evaporator used to dry Shaker herbs that he invented evaporated milk.

Shaker crafts are inspirational in a world where time-honored traditions and crafts are often overlooked. The following activities help today's children remember them.

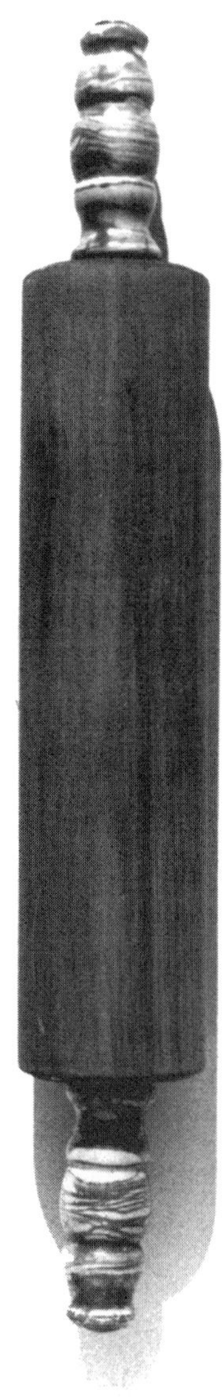

Cooking

Since everything the Shakers did showed their belief in simplicity and their desire to make only the best, Shaker food was always simple, basic, and well prepared.

Food preparation and the responsibility for the health and well-being of the Shaker families rested on the shoulders of the sisters. It was an enormous job to plan a healthy, interesting, and appetizing meal three times a day, every day of the year. It also required the preparation of a great amount of food to feed the hard-working Shaker families. Imagine how many loaves of bread and apple pies had to be baked every day to satisfy hungry men and women doing hard farm work. They needed to eat much more than people working at easier jobs. Nicholas Briggs, when he wrote about life in the Shaker village, remembered the fine quality and vast quantity of food set on the Shaker tables.

When feeding so many, the sisters had to be sure there were no mistakes made in food preparation. No dish set upon a Shaker table could be less than perfect. Waste of any kind went against the thrifty Shaker nature. Food simply could not be burned or improperly prepared. Shaker sisters had to achieve perfect results every time. So, in the days when all other cooks were adding a dash of this and a handful of that, they used very exact measurements and very scientific methods of food preparation.

They kept their families healthy by using sanitary procedures that were uncommon at the time. Shaker sisters were among the first Americans to study the nutritional value of food. They cooked vegetables with the skins on and then used the cooking water, which contained valuable nutrients, to prepare soups and sauces. They recognized the value of preparing special, healthy diets for the elderly and sick.

Shaker cooks had to be businesslike and efficient about their work. They invented time-saving kitchen helps like the famous Canterbury Revolving Oven with shelves that rotated to circulate heat evenly and made it possible to bake a great number of pies at the same time.

And they were pioneers in the science of preserving foods. Their clean and efficient canning kitchens provided the model for America's first canning factories.

While accomplishing all of these tasks, the sisters were still able to prepare incredibly delicious foods with many of the special twists we expect from today's finest restaurants. Recipes with names like Spinach with Rosemary and Sister Abigail's Blue Flower Omelet remind us of the special touch they gave everything they did. The creative Shaker sisters turned what could have been very ordinary food into a delicious cuisine flavored with fragrant herbs, spices, and delicate rose water. The following recipes are a sampling of a few specially prepared Shaker recipes. They have been changed a bit to bring them up to modern times.

Shaker Lemonade

Quantity • 6 glasses lemonade

Utensils

- Strainer
- Juice squeezer
- Bowl
- Metal measuring cups
- Large spoon
- Small knife
- Teakettle
- 2-quart pitcher
- Glasses

Ingredients

- 6 medium lemons
- 1 cup sugar
- 1 cup boiling water
- 2 quarts (8 cups) cold water
- Ice cubes
- Fresh mint leaves (optional)

Lemons do not grow in the northeastern United States where the first Shakers lived. But they were an important part of the early American diet because they were known to prevent a terrible disease called scurvy, which was very common several hundred years ago. The Shakers, who wanted to grow all of their own food, had to buy lemons from the outside world.

Shaker lemonade is like no other. Soaking the lemon rind in boiling water extracts fragrant lemon oil, which gives the lemonade a special flavor.

Directions *Requires adult assistance*

Step 1 • Squeeze each whole lemon in your hand to soften it and make it easier to remove the juice. With adult assistance, cut the lemons in half and squeeze the juice out through a strainer (to remove the pulp and seeds) into a pitcher. Stir in the sugar until it is completely dissolved.

Step 2 • Fill a teakettle with water and bring it to a boil over medium heat. Put the lemon rinds in a bowl and pour 1 cup of boiling water over them. Leave them in the bowl until the water cools.

Step 3 • Remove the lemon rinds from the bowl and add the water in the bowl to the juice and sugar in the pitcher. Stir well.

Step 4 • Add 8 cups of cold water to the pitcher and stir well. Put a few ice cubes in each glass and fill with lemonade. Garnish with mint leaves.

Shaker Daily Loaf

Bread is often called the staff of life. This means that it is the single most important and universal food. Bread was an important food for the Shakers, too. At each meal, a plate of delicious fresh bread was placed in the center of each square. Nicholas Briggs was taught to Shaker his plate after every meal with a piece of bread.

All Shaker bread was handmade by the sisters in the kitchen. To make a good loaf of bread requires time and patience. It is wonderful to feel the soft dough in your hands, to smell the fragrance of baking bread in the oven, and to see the golden loaf cooling in the kitchen. Enjoyable as bread making is, it must have been a big job to mix, knead, and bake enough bread to feed a family of more than one hundred.

The sisters used Shaker-milled flour, which contained the valuable nutrients from the wheat germ. Today's flour may be too processed to provide the same nutrition. The addition of wheat germ makes a healthier bread.

Quantity • 1 large loaf white bread
Preparation time • 3 hours
Oven temperature • 350°
Baking time • Check after 30 minutes

Utensils

Metal measuring cups
Measuring spoons
Large mixing bowl
Medium saucepan
Glass measuring cup
Clean kitchen towel
Bread pan, 9⅝" x 5½" x 2¾"
Hot pads
Cooling rack

Ingredients

2 cups milk
¼ cup warm water
1 packet active dry yeast
2 tablespoons butter
2 tablespoons sugar
2 teaspoons salt
1 tablespoon wheat germ
4 cups unbleached white flour
1½ to 2 cups additional flour

Directions *Requires adult assistance*

Step 1 • Measure 2 cups of milk in a glass measuring cup and pour it into a saucepan. Check your measurement while the measuring cup is sitting on a level surface and you are looking at eye level. Set the pan aside and wash out the measuring cup.

Step 2 • Run the kitchen faucet until the water is warm, not hot, and fill the glass measuring cup with ¼ cup warm water. Check the expiration date on the yeast package before emptying yeast into the water. Stir until the yeast dissolves. Yeast is a living culture and it will grow best when it is slightly warm. Set the

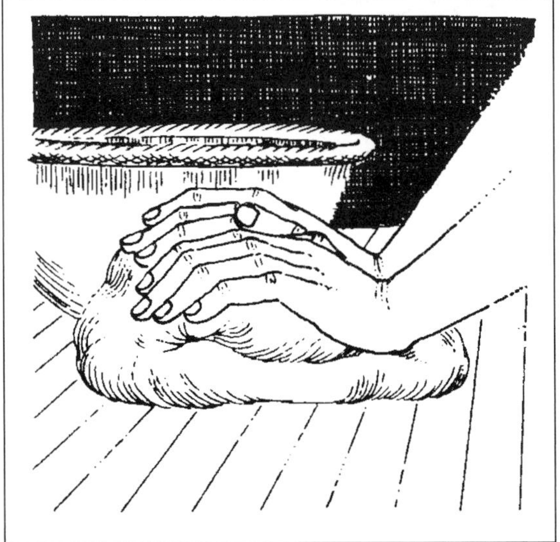

measuring cup in a warmish, draft-free place. The oven of a gas stove is a good place to put the measuring cup. The oven may be warmed to 150°, but it must be shut off when the yeast is placed inside.

Step 3 • Place the saucepan on the stove and turn it on low. Stir the milk occasionally until a thin skin forms on the surface of the milk and bubbles begin to form around the edges. Heat will kill bacteria in the milk that might harm the yeast.

Step 4 • Measure the butter and add it to the hot milk. Stir until the butter is dissolved. Measure the sugar, salt, and wheat germ and stir them into the milk and butter. Allow the mixture to cool until you can comfortably stick your finger into the mixture.

Step 5 • Check the yeast and water mixture. All the grains of yeast should be dissolved and turned into a thick, putty-gray mass with bubbles on top. If the yeast does not look like this, throw it away and start again. If the yeast is not alive and growing, your bread will not rise and it will be a dense, heavy, disappointing failure.

Step 6 • Stir the yeast into the cooled milk mixture. Beat in 4 cups of flour, 1 cup at a time. An electric mixer helps with this job. Allow the dough to rest for 10 minutes. This will make it easier to knead.

Step 7 • If your bowl is very large and roomy, you can knead the bread in the bowl. Or you may lightly flour a clean countertop and put the dough on it. Sprinkle 1 cup of flour over the dough and begin to knead as follows: Starting with the edge of dough closest to you, push the dough away from you lightly with the heels of your hands. Now pull the outside edges over the top of the dough. Turn the dough a quarter-turn and repeat the same motions. Continue pushing, pulling, and turning the dough in a nice steady rhythm.

Step 8 • After you have completely kneaded in the first cup of flour, sprinkle and knead in ½ cup of flour at a time. As the dough becomes less sticky, it will feel smooth and elastic. Air bubbles will begin to form on the surface. The amount of flour needed to finish the dough will vary from one batch of bread to another. Kneading the dough is important because it completes the mixing of the ingredients and develops the structure that holds the bread together. Normal kneading time is about 12 minutes.

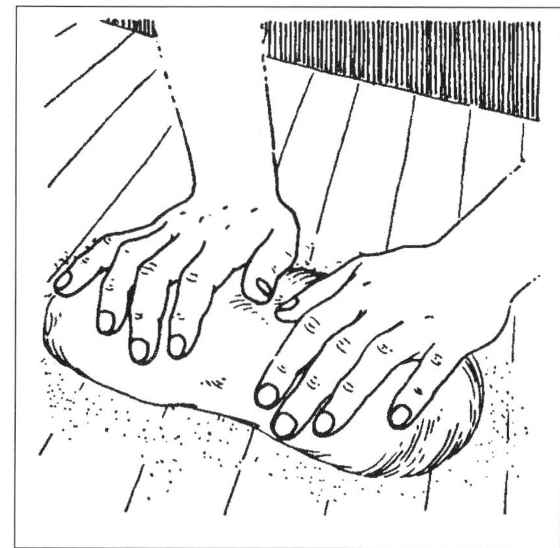

Step 9 • Lightly grease the sides of the mixing bowl with the extra butter. Wet a clean kitchen towel and squeeze out the excess water. The towel must not be drippy. Put the dough in the bowl and cover it with the damp towel. Place the bowl in a warm, draft-free place (shut-off oven, for example), and leave it until the dough has doubled in size. This should take about an hour.

Step 10 • Punch the dough down by pressing your fist through it to the bottom of the bowl. Fold the edges of the dough over from all four sides and punch the dough down a second time. Let the dough rest for 10 minutes while you prepare the bread pan.

Step 11 • Generously butter the entire inside of a bread pan. Form the dough into a loaf shape and put it in the pan. Place the pan in a warm, draft-free place and leave it untouched until the dough has again doubled in size.

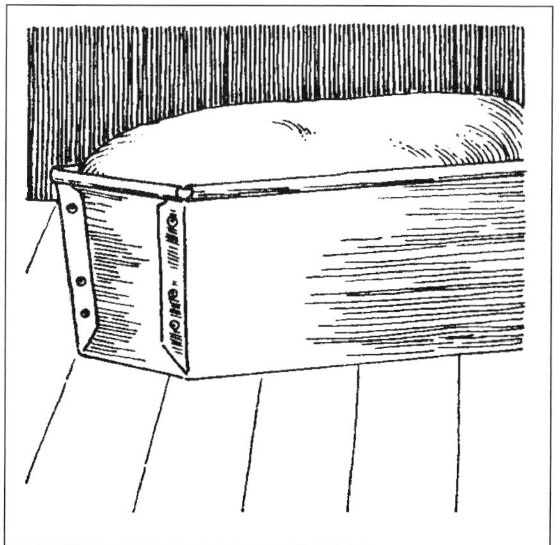

Step 12 • Place the pan in the center of a 350° oven and bake for ½ hour. Check the bread. If the top is a lovely deep, golden-brown color, the bread is ready to remove from the oven and cool on a rack. Let the bread cool for at least 20 minutes before cutting it with a serrated knife.

Berry Jam

Shaker jelly labels.

Both Nicholas Briggs and Anita Potter enjoyed picking berries, and they usually picked more than they could eat. The extra berries were taken home to the sisters. In those days there were no home freezers and no frozen-food sections at the supermarket. To preserve the fresh berries, the sisters made jelly and jam.

There is special magic in making your own jam. First there is the challenge of finding the fresh fruit. Then there is the wonderful smell of the fruit cooking in your kitchen, and later the reassuring pop of the lids as they seal on the jars. Finally, the beautifully colored mason jars lined up on your kitchen shelf are enough to make any cook and helper burst with pride.

If you are lucky enough to live in the country, you may know where wild berries grow. Be sure to ask permission before you pick berries growing on someone else's land. If you live in the city, purchase berries in the spring and early summer at one of the weekly outdoor farmer's markets. Or ask a parent to help you find a farmer who will permit a farm visit and allow you to pick his or her berries. If none of these ideas will work for your family, a local supermarket will have enough fresh berries to make several jars of jam almost any time of the year.

Quantity • 2 ½-pint jars of berry jelly

Preparation time • 1 hour

Utensils

1-gallon heavy-duty kettle
Small kettle
Large spoon
Set of measuring cups
2 large hot pads
Clean paper toweling
Kitchen thermometer
Colander
Kitchen tongs
2 ½-pint mason jars, bands, and new lids

Ingredients

2 cups of fresh berries — boysenberries, blackberries, raspberries, or strawberries
½ cup water
1 package pectin (for strawberry jelly only)
2 cups white sugar

Directions *Requires adult assistance*

Step 1 • Examine the rims of the mason jars for chips. If the rims are chipped, the lids will not seal to the jar. Wash the jars and lids in warm soapy water, rinse, and dry.

Step 2 • Put the berries in a colander and gently wash them with water. Pick out and discard any moldy or very soft berries. Remove all stems from the berries. Put the berries in the large kettle and add ½ cup water. Cook over medium heat until the berries are crushed by the heat and give off juice. Remove the pan from the heat and allow the berries to cool to lukewarm. If you are using strawberries, you will need to add a little artificial pectin to thicken the fruit. Follow the directions for using pectin on the package.

Step 3 • Pour the berries and juice into a bowl. Measure 2 cups and return to the large kettle. Measure 2 cups of white sugar and stir until dissolved in the berries and juice. At the same time, fill a smaller kettle half full of water and put the clean jars, bands, and lids in the water. Put the kettle on the stove and heat until the water begins to boil. This will sterilize the jars. Put the kettle containing the berries, liquid, and sugar back on the stove and turn the heat on high. Attach the kitchen thermometer to the side of the kettle. Gently and continuously stir the berries until they begin to bubble and boil. When the thermometer reaches 220° the jam is done. Remove the kettle from the stove.

Step 4 • Use kitchen tongs to take the jars out of the hot water and turn them upside-down on the paper toweling. Remove the lids and bands from the kettle with the tongs and put them on the paper toweling.

Step 5 • Skim any whitish foam from the top of the jam with a spoon and discard it. Use the ladle to fill the jars almost to the top with the very hot jam. Wipe any drips from the rims with a damp, clean paper towel and immediately seal the jars with the lids and bands. Use a hot pad to hold the jar while you tighten the bands. Put the hot jars of jelly on a windowsill to cool. As the jam cools, a vacuum will be formed inside the jar and the lid will make a popping sound as it tightens in place. When the jars are cool, check the lids for a small indentation in the center. If the indentation is there, you have successfully sealed the jar and it may be stored in a cool dark place until you are ready to use it. If the center of the lid is wiggly to the touch, the jar is not sealed and must be stored in the refrigerator.

Step 6 • Make two labels and neatly attach them to the jars. Directions for making labels are given on page 80.

Canterbury Applesauce

The Canterbury Shakers were famous for the delicious apples grown in their orchards. In the days before it was possible to preserve fruit with canning, they made a very special applesauce. Small and imperfect apples were carefully peeled, cut, dried in large ovens, and put in storage. Whenever the sisters needed a new batch of applesauce, the dried apples were taken out of storage, soaked in water, and cooked in Shaker-made apple cider. This applesauce was very different from the applesauce we know today.

Today we are able to get fresh apples all year-round and we do not make applesauce from dried apples. The very unusual flavor and texture of dried apples makes this recipe worth remembering.

Directions *Requires adult assistance*

Step 1 • Put the dried apples in a bowl and cover them with water. Soak overnight.

Step 2 • Put the apples, remaining water, and concentrated apple juice in the 4-quart heavy saucepan. Cook for 20 minutes. Add sugar and cinnamon to taste. Serve when cool.

Quantity • 2 cups applesauce

Preparation time • ½ hour + soaking

Utensils

4-quart heavy saucepan
Metal measuring cups
Bowl

Ingredients

½ pound dried apples
1 cup concentrated canned apple juice
½ cup sugar (optional)
Cinnamon

Shaker Baked Apple Dumplings

Quantity • 6 servings
Preparation time • 2 hours
Oven temperature • 350°
Baking time • 30 minutes

Apples were a main ingredient in the Shaker diet and apple pie the most common dessert served at the Shaker table. Nicholas Briggs fondly remembered eating more than half an apple pie at one sitting. This recipe for baked apple dumplings is a tasty Shaker alternative to apple pie.

Utensils

- Pyrex baking dish (approximately 6" x 9" x 2")
- Apple peeler and corer or small paring knife
- Measuring spoons
- Metal measuring cups
- Glass measuring cup
- Turkey baster
- Pastry cutter or 2 knives
- Pastry cloth
- Rolling pin
- 2-quart saucepan
- Mixing bowl
- Waxed paper
- Fork

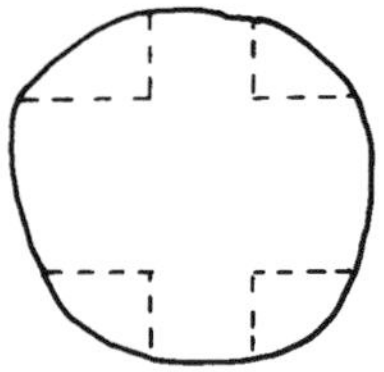

Directions *Requires adult assistance*

Step 1 • Measure all crust ingredients except milk and put them in a mixing bowl. Cut the butter into the dry ingredients using a pastry cutter or 2 knives, until the pieces of butter are no larger than a pea. Use the turkey baster to sprinkle cold milk over the ingredients in the bowl. Knead lightly with hands only until dough and milk are mixed together. Divide into 6 balls of equal size. Wrap each ball in waxed paper and refrigerate for one hour.

Step 2 • Measure sugar and water and put them in a saucepan. Cook over medium heat for 5 minutes or until the mixture begins to boil. Remove from heat and stir in nutmeg, cinnamon, and butter.

Step 3: assembly • Peel and core the apples. Roll out the chilled dough, one ball at a time. Dough should be about ⅛-inch thick and a circular size large enough to wrap completely around an apple. Cut out the corners as illustrated at left. Sprinkle the dough with a little cinnamon and place an apple in the center. Fill the hole in the center of the apple with brown sugar and a tablespoon of butter. Wrap the dough around the apple and press it together at the top. Prick through the dough with a fork. Set the finished dumpling aside and wrap the other apples, one at a time. Arrange apples in a baking dish. Spoon sauce or maple syrup over apples. Place on a rack in the middle of the oven and bake for approximately ½ hour or until the crust is golden brown, basting apples with sauce one time during baking. Serve warm.

Ingredients

6 medium-sized tart apples

Crust

1 cup white flour

1 cup pastry flour (white or whole wheat)

2 teaspoons baking powder

¾ cup cold butter

1 teaspoon salt

½ cup cold milk

Sauce

2 cups sugar

2 cups water

¼ teaspoon nutmeg

¼ teaspoon cinnamon

¼ cup butter

Or you may use

2 cups maple syrup

¼ cup butter

Extra Ingredients

Cinnamon or rose water

Brown sugar

6 tablespoons butter

Shaker Candy

Materials

One recipe home-made candy
Candy wrapping paper
Small candy boxes
Ribbon

The Shaker sisters made many different kinds of candy to sell to the world. Of course, the Shaker candy was attractively packaged before it was offered for sale. You may purchase fancy candy wrappers and small cardboard boxes from cake and candy supply stores. Make some labels, (page 80) and wrap up your home-made candy to give as a gift.

Right: Tabletop filled with Shaker-made candy.
Below: Shaker candy label.

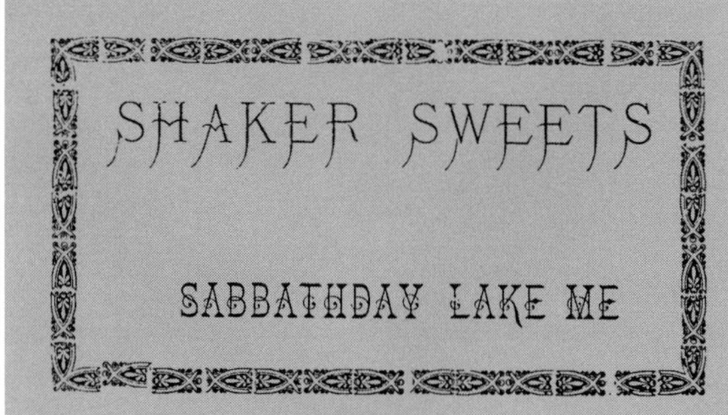

Old-Fashioned Caramel

Quantity • 2¼ pounds candy
Preparation time • 1 hour

When sugar and a liquid are boiled together, a syrup is formed that grows thicker as the boiling continues. The thickness of the syrup determines the kind of candy made from it. Because the temperature of the syrup rises steadily as it thickens, the simplest and best way to make sure your candy will turn out perfectly is to measure the temperature of the syrup with a thermometer as it cooks.

Utensils

- 2-quart heavy saucepan
- Metal measuring cups
- Measuring spoons
- Glass measuring cup
- Buttered sheet-cake pan
- Candy thermometer
- Electric mixer

Ingredients

- 3 cups sugar
- 1½ cups heavy cream
- 2 cups white Karo syrup
- 1½ tablespoons vanilla

Directions *Requires adult assistance*

Step 1 • Measure and stir sugar, heavy cream, and corn syrup in a heavy 2-quart pan until blended.

Step 2 • Cook over medium to high heat with the candy thermometer inserted in pan. Stir occasionally until the mixture reaches the firm boil stage, 248°.

Step 3 • Remove from heat and cool to lukewarm. Add vanilla and beat with an electric mixer until the shiny look disappears and the caramel holds its shape when dropped from a spoon.

Step 4 • Turn out into a buttered cake pan and cut into squares.

Fireside Treats: Roasted Chestnuts and Popcorn

Utensils

- Fine-mesh wire basket with a long handle for cooking over an open fire
- Firewood and kindling
- Old hot pads
- Metal measuring cups
- 2 metal serving bowls
- Paper towels
- Hot or cold drinks
- Chairs or blankets

Ingredients

- ½ pound fresh chestnuts
- ½ cup popcorn kernels
- Salt
- Melted butter or oil (optional)

Roasted nuts gathered in the woods and popcorn grown on Boys' Island were a special treat for Nicholas Briggs. If you live in a house with a fireplace, you can roast nuts and pop corn with adult supervision in your living room. Or your family can go on an outing and build a campfire. Enjoy nature, tell stories, and sing songs while you roast your fireside treats.

Directions *Requires adult assistance*

Step 1 • Plan when and where to build the cooking fire with an adult. Build and light the fire only with adult supervision.

Step 2 • When the fire is ready, put the chestnuts in the wire basket and hold them over the fire until they become hot and pop. Remove them from the basket using the hot pads and put them in a bowl until they cool enough to peel and eat.

Step 3 • Put ½ cup popcorn in the basket and hold it over the fire until all of the popcorn pops. Put the popcorn in the second bowl and add salt and butter to taste. Serve with hot or cold drinks and pass the bowls. Enjoy the feeling of community and friendship shared around an open fire while telling stories or singing songs.

Step 4 • Make sure the fire is extinguished when you are ready to leave.

Plants and Gardens

Vegetable gardens and orchards were an important part of every Shaker village because Mother Ann directed her followers to be self-sufficient. This meant the Shakers had to grow all of their own food. They replaced foods they could not grow themselves with foods they could grow. For example, rose water flavoring made from village-grown flowers was used in place of vanilla. Lemons, a rare exception, were purchased from the world because they were considered necessary for good health.

The Shakers worked hard and grew wonderful gardens. They used all they needed and sold the rest. They not only had more vegetables than they could use, but they also had too many seeds. Not wanting to waste the extra seeds, they sold them to the world as early as 1789. At first, the seeds were sold from large containers by the pound. This worked for farmers, but some people wanted only a few seeds. The inventive Shakers prepared seeds for home gardens in small paper packages and became the first to sell packaged seeds. This business quickly grew into the Shakers' first big industry. In the early 1800s eleven Shaker villages were making a good profit from the sale of packaged seeds.

Today vegetables and fruits may be purchased at the local supermarket. It is easy for us to forget the joy and hard work that once went into the daily preparation of food. Old-fashioned recipes, wildflower collections, and gardens help us remember what life was like a long time ago.

Utensils

Wooden frame approximately 24" square (this could be made from canvas stretchers purchased at the art supply store)
Cheesecloth
Tacks and tack hammer
1-quart glass jar with tight-fitting lid
Mortar and pestle
Orris root powder (optional)
Waxed paper
Measuring spoons
Large glass container with tight-fitting lid

Potpourri

Fragrant potpourri made with herbs and flowers from the Shaker gardens is still sold by the Sabbathday Lake Shakers.

To make your own potpourri, choose ingredients from the materials list depending on the time of year and what grows where you live.

Directions *Requires adult assistance*

Step 1 • Stretch cheesecloth over the frame and tack it firmly to the sides to make a drying rack for the flowers.

Step 2 • Collect fresh flower petals and herbs and carefully spread them on the drying rack. The flowers should not touch each other. Put them in a dry shaded place where air circulates freely until they are completely dry to the touch. This may take a week to ten days.

Step 3 • At the same time, prepare dried peel. Carefully peel only the outer skin of the fruit, avoiding the white inner layer. Dipping the peel in orris root powder before drying will intensify the scent. Spread the peel out on waxed paper and put in a dry place until it is dry to the touch. You will need 4 tablespoons of dried citrus peel to make the potpourri.

Step 4 • When the flowers, herbs, and citrus peel are dried, you are ready to make the potpourri. Grind 1 teaspoon of spices from the materials list with a mortar and pestle or a pepper mill.

Step 5 • Sprinkle a ½-inch layer of dried flowers on the bottom of the glass container and cover with a sprinkling of salt. Sprinkle ½ teaspoon of ground spices and 1 tablespoon of dried citrus peel over the flower petals.

Add three more layers of flower petals, herbs, salt, spices, and citrus peel and the jar is ready to seal tightly. Store it in a dark place for two weeks. Open and stir. Reseal and store in a dark place for six to eight weeks, stirring one time every week.

Step 6 • Use the potpourri to fill small fragrant pillows made from scraps of fabrics. Follow the directions for Fir Balsam Pillows, page 114, substituting colorful scraps of fabric for the transparent fabric. Or display your colorful potpourri in a pretty dish.

Materials

(choose a few from each list)

Fresh flower petals

Rose, lavender, lemon verbena, rose geranium, delphinium, phlox, calendula, lilac, lily of the valley, hyacinth, jasmine, mock orange, narcissus, nicotiana, orange blossom, violet, marigold, or pansy

Fresh herbs

Basil, bay, bergamot, lemon verbena, mint, rosemary, sage, sweet marjoram, sweet woodruff, tarragon, thyme, dill, or anise

Whole spices

Allspice, cinnamon, cloves, nutmeg, cardamom, ginger, vanilla pods, anise, or mace

Dried peel

Orange, lemon, grapefruit, or lime

Salt

Materials

Bucket with a handle to carry flowers
Notebook
Book of local wildflowers for identification
Pencils and pens for drawing
Camera
Book with blank pages
Newspapers
Several heavy books
Name tags for the flowers
Water-based glue

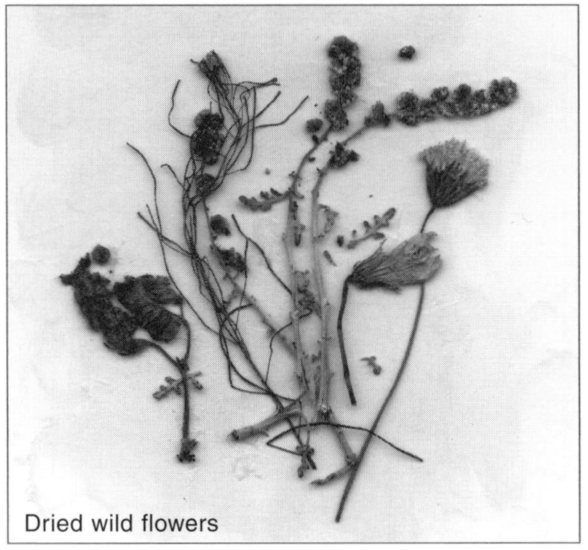
Dried wild flowers

A Wildflower Collection

Anita Potter collected, identified, and preserved more than two hundred different wildflowers and won first prize at the Hancock Fair. It is still fun to spend a spring or summer day hunting for wildflowers. Be sure to learn which species are endangered and protected by law. Don't pick these flowers, just write them down and sketch them in your notebook or photograph them. Remember, never pick a wildflower if it is the only one.

Directions

Step 1 • Set aside a special spring or summer day to go on your wildflower hunt. Pack your supplies in a book bag and dress for a day in the woods and fields. Choose a place to hike where picking flowers is permitted.

Step 2 • Gather wildflowers and put them in water in the bucket to keep them fresh. Remember, don't pick a flower if it is the only one. Always leave a few flowers behind to reseed for next season. Use the book to identify the flowers you find.

Step 3 • Carefully arrange flowers on several thicknesses of newspaper, labeling each one with a pen. Cover them with more layers of newspaper and weigh down with several heavy books. Leave the flowers like this for two weeks.

Step 4 • Carefully remove flowers from newspaper and glue them on the pages of a blank book, one species of flower per page. Label neatly.

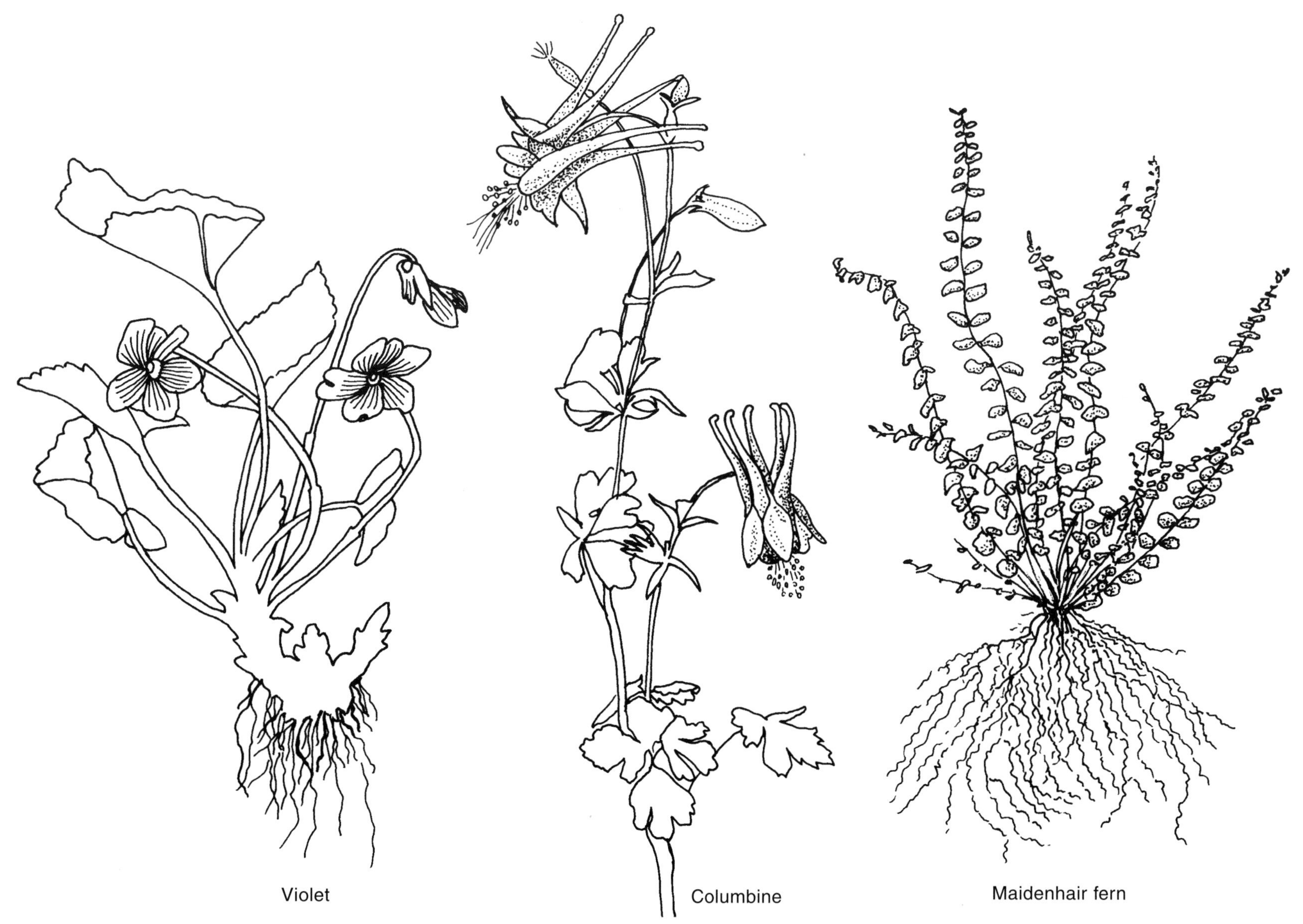
Violet
Columbine
Maidenhair fern

A Vegetable Garden

Materials

- Pencil and paper
- 10′ x 10′ plot of ground, approved by parents
- Spade
- Rake
- Garden gloves
- 6 grape stakes, 5′ in length
- Several smaller stakes for the tomatoes
- Garden twine
- 2 tomato seedlings
- Package of seeds for green beans, climbing or pole variety
- 4 parsley plants
- 10 marigold plants, a natural insect repellent
- Package of seeds for pumpkins
- Package of seeds for sunflowers
- 5-pound sack of fertilizer (check with a local nursery for the correct type and amount)
- Package of ladybugs or a praying mantis egg case (fun! but optional)
- Basket

Nicholas Briggs was pleased to be given the important responsibility of working in the main garden. Ask your parents for a small piece of the yard to try your hand at growing vegetables.

If you live in an apartment or your yard is too small for a vegetable garden, try growing green bush bean seeds in medium-sized flowerpots.

Directions *Requires adult permission and assistance*

Step 1 • In the spring, when the ground is moist (neither dry nor soaking wet), dig up the garden plot and break up lumps in the soil. This will take work. When you are finished, the soil should be fine and slip easily through your fingers. Remove stones and weeds by raking over the surface. Sprinkle fertilizer evenly over the plot and turn the soil over one more time to work fertilizer in.

Step 2 • Make a drawing of your planting scheme with pencil and paper. A sample garden is shown on the next page. Be sure to leave a lot of room for the plants and seeds to grow.

Step 3 • Plant the garden following your plan. Make a mound of dirt 3 feet across for the pumpkin seeds. Make two teepees with the grape stakes, using three stakes per teepee, and tie them together at the top. Plant the bean seeds at the bottom of the teepees. Carefully remove the parsley, tomato, and marigold plants from the pots and transplant them.

Step 4 • Check on your garden every day. When it looks dry, water it gently with a hose. If it looks like something is feasting on your plants, look

tomatoes
pumpkins
beans
parsley
marigolds
sunflowers

A successful young gardener stands in front of his nine foot sunflowers.

for bugs. Ask a local nursery for help in fighting the bugs. It is helpful to take a sample of the bug or a leaf that has been nibbled to the nursery. Ladybugs and praying mantis egg cases released in your garden are fun to watch and useful because they eat harmful insects.

The pumpkin seeds will send up hearty shoots and then grow vines. Train the vines away from your other plants. Use small plastic strawberry baskets to prop the pumpkins up off the ground. Carefully turn them so they will develop on all sides.

When the tomato plants are 18 inches high they will need to be staked. Circular tomato towers made from wire are useful, but several garden stakes will do as well.

Step 5 • After a few weeks, you will begin to harvest from your garden. A basket will be helpful for carrying the vegetables and flowers to the house. Here are some harvesting tips.

Parsley • The parsley may be snipped off a little at a time. Don't cut the entire plant as it will continue growing for up to a year.

Beans • The beans should be ready to eat in five weeks. Harvest beans when they are about three inches long. The beans are too big when the seeds are protruding lumps along the sides of the beans. Pick the beans often. The more beans you pick, the more you will get.

Pumpkins • Pumpkins are ready for harvest when they have turned a beautiful orange color.

Tomatoes • When the tomatoes are red, they are ready for picking.

Marigolds • The flowers are there to enjoy. Pick a few as a special gift for a parent or friend. Dry them to use in potpourri.

Sunflowers • When the petals fall from the flowers, hang the flower heads from a tree for the birds and squirrels to feast on.

Paper Crafts

Shaker children enjoyed making things with paper. They were thrifty and used the supplies they had at home. Some of the things they made are part of museum collections today.

Shaker Valentines

Materials

- Scissors
- Colored construction or origami paper
- Ribbon scraps
- Stickers and old valentines to cut apart
- Colored pencils or pens
- Package of heart-shaped doilies
- Glue stick

In the 1840s, several Shaker girls made Shaker valentines they called messages of love from Mother Ann. They drew heart- and leaf-shaped valentines for every member of the family and left them on the breakfast table in the early morning. This is a charming sentiment and one you may like to try, even when it is not February 14.

Directions

Trace these hearts and cut them out. Paste each heart in the center of a heart-shaped doily. Decorate each valentines with ribbons and stickers.

May Baskets

The ancient custom of anonymously leaving May baskets filled with fresh spring flowers on doorknobs has all but been forgotten. It is a nice way to remember a relative, neighbor, or an elderly friend.

Materials

- Several sheets of heavy paper
- Scissors
- Ruler
- Pencil
- Several paper fasteners
- Paper punch
- Fresh spring flowers with at least 8-inch stems
- Plastic florist's vials
- Glue stick

Directions *Requires adult assistance*

Step 1 • Make a list of three or four people you would like to remember with a May basket.

Step 2 • Pick or purchase flowers on April 30 to fill each basket on your list with six to eight flowers. Remove bottom leaves from the stems of the flowers. Fill the vials with water, cover with plastic top, and put one or two flowers in each vial. You will need three or four flower-filled vials for each May basket. Store the flowers in a cool place overnight.

Step 3 • Cut several 12″ circles from paper and cut them in half. Glue the sides of each half-circle together to form a cone. Cut a handle for each basket, 2″ x 12″. Fold the handles in half lengthwise for added strength. Attach the handles to the cones with two paper fasteners. Get up early in the morning on May 1. Arrange flowers in May baskets and take an adult with you to hang them on doorknobs.

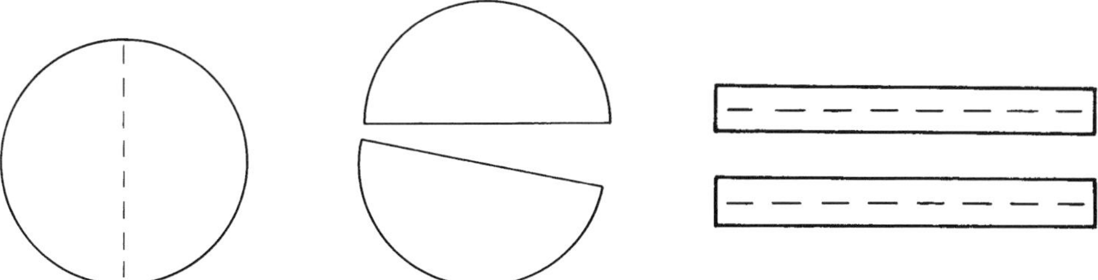

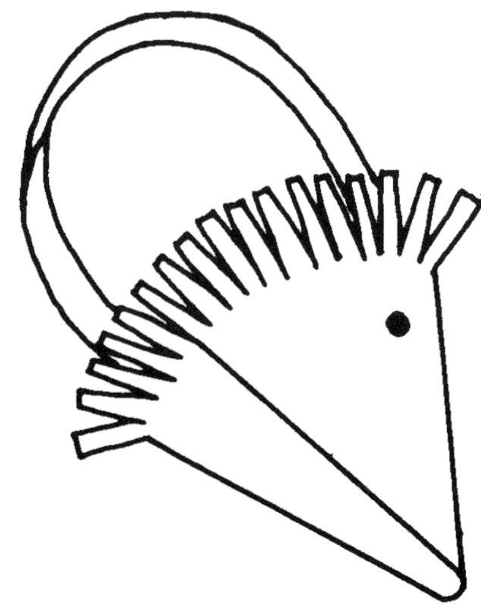

Materials

- Several sheets of heavy white paper, 8½" x 11"
- Scissors
- Ruler
- Tracing paper and soft pencil
- Colored pens
- Glue stick
- 1 pressure-sensitive white label for each jar of jam

Jam Labels and Seed Packets

Draw a picture of the berry you used to make the jam in pencil on each label. Color your drawings with colored pens. Write the name of the jam, your name, and the date you made it in black on the label.

Trace the shape shown below and transfer it to white paper (Step 1, page 81). Cut the seed packet out. Draw and color a vegetable on the front of the packet. Fold and glue the packet together as illustrated.

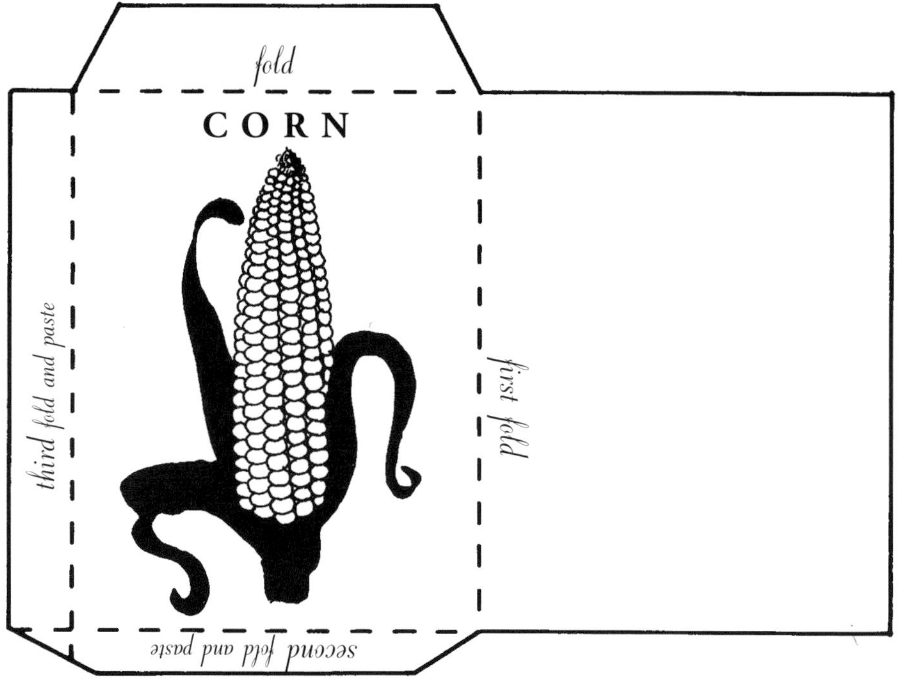

Halloween Lanterns

The entire Hancock family joined in the preparations for the Halloween activity. The basement kitchen was decorated and turned into a witches' den. These paper lanterns will look spooky in your house.

Materials

- Extra-heavy black paper
- Sheet of orange tissue paper
- Scissors
- 8- or 10-penny common nail
- Hammer
- Small block of wood
- Ruler and pencil
- Compass
- Tracing paper and soft pencil (optional)
- Tape
- White glue and paper clips
- Small battery-operated light source

Directions

Step 1 • Measure and draw the two pattern pieces on black paper. Cut lantern pieces out with the scissors. Put the block of wood under the pattern pieces and use the hammer and nail to punch star-like holes in the paper. Trace the Halloween cat or witch from page 77. Turn the tracing paper over and color over the line with the side of the soft pencil. Sharpen the pencil. Turn the paper right side up and position it on the lantern. Draw over the lines of the design with the pencil a second time to transfer the design to the lantern.

Step 2 • Carefully cut the design out. Cut a piece of tissue paper big enough to cover the design and tape it to the back of the paper. Glue the short sides of the lantern together using paper clips to hold the paper in place while the glue dries. Glue the half-circle together. Place the lantern over a small battery-operated light source and set the top on it.

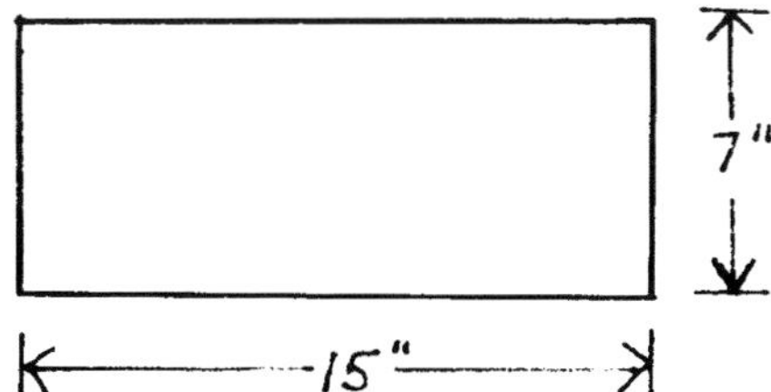

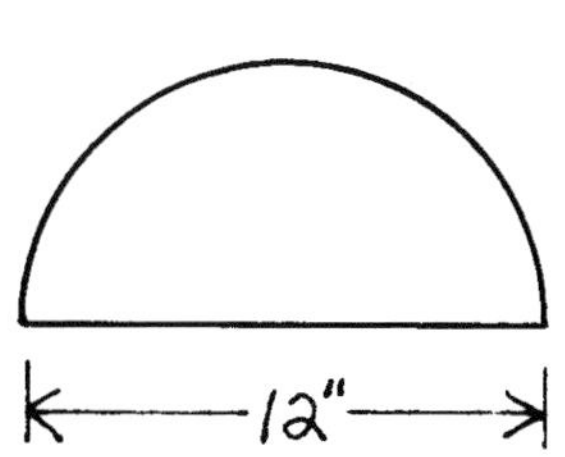

Thanksgiving Placecards

Materials

- Several sheets of white paper if you are using a computer
- Blank white 5" x 7" index cards
- Scissors
- Colored construction paper
- Colored pencils and pens

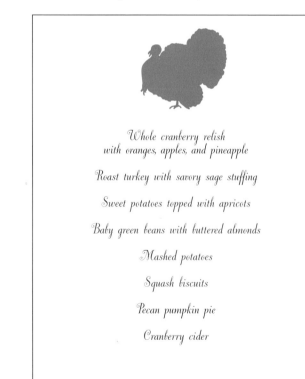

Whole cranberry relish with oranges, apples, and pineapple

Roast turkey with savory sage stuffing

Sweet potatoes topped with apricots

Baby green beans with buttered almonds

Mashed potatoes

Squash biscuits

Pecan pumpkin pie

Cranberry cider

When Nicholas Briggs lived at Canterbury, holidays were barely observed. But during Anita Potter's time at Hancock, they were joyfully celebrated. Shaker children made decorated menus for Thanksgiving dinner and other holidays. Plan to do this activity about one week before Thanksgiving. You may wish to do it for other special family dinners, too.

Directions

Step 1 • Ask your parents to write down the Thanksgiving menu for you. Be sure to include all the special details about the food. For example, instead of saying "cranberry sauce" and "green beans," you will want to say "whole cranberry sauce" and "green beans with slivered almonds and butter."

Step 2 • Carefully print the menu in the center of the card. Use a new line for each food. Or you may type the menu on a computer and trim the printout to fit in the center of your menu placecards. Write each guest's name at the top of a card in a different color. Cut decorations out of colored paper and paste them on the index cards.

Woven Christmas Ornaments

Anita Potter admired the woven Shaker chair seats when she worked in the dining room with Anna Delcheff. These woven tree ornaments are an easier way to learn about the craft of chair weaving.

Materials

- Several pieces of white paper
- Scissors
- Red and green construction paper or several 6″ x 6″ squares of metallic origami paper
- Colored pens
- Ruler
- Paper punch

Directions

Step 1 • From the red construction paper, cut six strips, 1″ x 10″. From the green construction paper, cut six strips, 1″ x 12″.

Step 2 • Place a white sheet of paper on a table and tape the red paper strips side by side to the paper using masking tape as illustrated. In weaving, these strips are called the warp.

Step 3 • Weave the green strips through the red strips. In weaving, these strips are called the weft or woof.

Step 4 • Glue the strips to the paper all around the sides. Use the scissors to cut the woven square out of the paper. Punch a hole in one corner and thread a piece of ribbon through it. Tie the ribbon in a knot and the paper weaving is ready to hang on the Christmas tree.

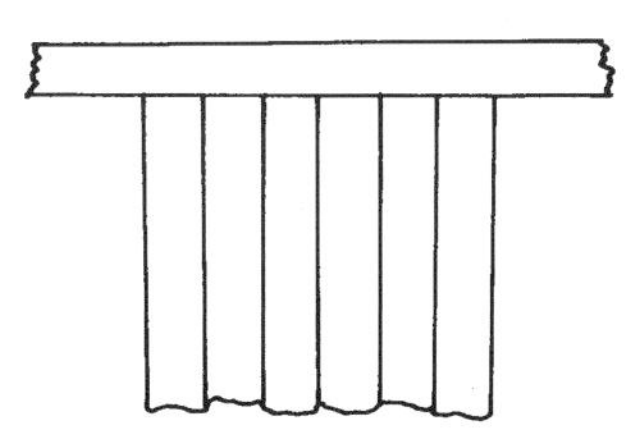

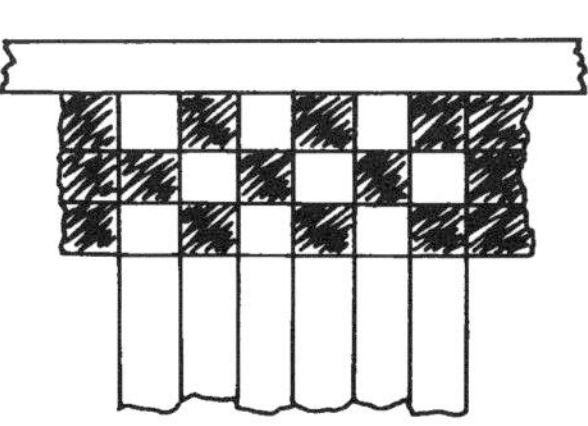

Games and Toys

Although Shaker children played the same games as the world's children, they had less time to play. In 1852, Nicholas Briggs was not allowed toys of his own. The few toys in the Canterbury Boys' House belonged to everyone. The Shaker rules had changed by 1925 when Anita Potter went to live at Hancock village. Shaker children were allowed to keep their own toys. And in those years the children probably helped the sisters make fancywork toys to sell to the world.

Marbles and Jacks: Games and a Bag

Children in the late 1800s played games with marbles and jacks.

Marble Game

Each player has a bag filled with many small marbles and one large marble called a "shooter." The players draw a large chalk circle at least 5 feet in diameter on the ground and mark the center with a large cross. Each player contributes 4 to 8 small marbles to the center of the circle, depending on the number of players. No more than 16 small marbles are placed on the cross in the center of the circle. The object of the game is to be the first to knock 7 marbles out of the circle.

Round 1 • The first player marks a shooting spot on the ring of the circle with his name. He then shoots one of his marbles from his shooting spot, trying to hit the marbles in the center of the circle. If he misses, he loses his turn. If he is successful, he continues shooting until he misses. After the first shot, shooters are played from where they stop within the circle. When the first player misses and loses his turn, his shooter is returned to his shooting spot.

Round 2 • The second player takes her turn in the same manner until she misses a shot and the turn passes to player 3.

Round 3 to end • The first player to knock 7 marbles out of the circle wins the game and the marbles she knocked out of the circle.

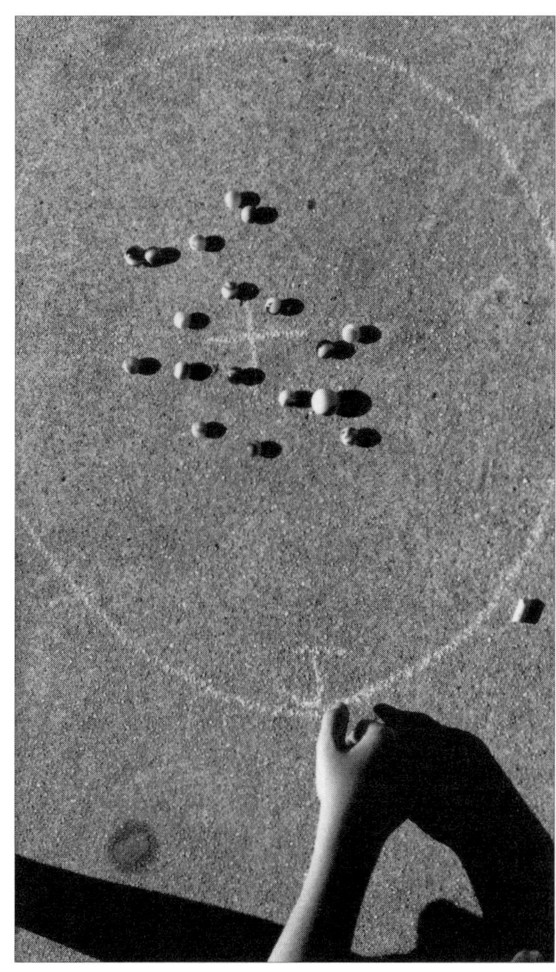

Jacks

Each player has 10 jacks and a small ball. The object of the game is to be the first to pick all of the jacks off the floor, playing by the following rules.

Round 1 • The first player throws all of her jacks on the floor. At the same time, she bounces the ball once and picks up one jack before catching the ball. This jack is put aside and the action is repeated until she has picked up all of her jacks. If she successfully completes round 1, she continues to round 2. If she misses at any time the turn passes to player 2.

Player 2 throws his jacks on the floor. At the same time, he bounces the ball once and picks up one jack before catching the ball. These jacks are put aside and the action is repeated until he has picked up all of his jacks. If he misses at any time the turn passes back to player 1. If he successfully completes round 1, he continues to round 2.

Round 2 • Player 1 throws her jacks on the floor. At the same time, she bounces the ball once and picks up two jacks before catching the ball. These jacks are put aside and the process repeated until she picks up all of her jacks. If she misses at any time the turn passes to player 2. If she successfully completes round 2, she continues to round 3.

Round 3 to end • The game continues in the same manner until one player has picked up all of her jacks successfully. When a player misses, he must pass the turn to the next player. When it is his turn again, he must go back to the beginning of the round he missed.

A Bag

Materials

Small piece of chamois
Scissors
Ruler, pencil, and paper
Leather shoelace
Sewing machine and thread

Directions

Draw a paper pattern and cut two pieces of chamois 3″ x 4″. Machine- sew around 3 sides. Turn the bag inside out. With the scissors cut two small holes on both sides of the bag about 1″ from the open end. Cut two 10″ lengths from the leather shoelaces and thread them through the holes. Knot the ends together and the bag is ready to use.

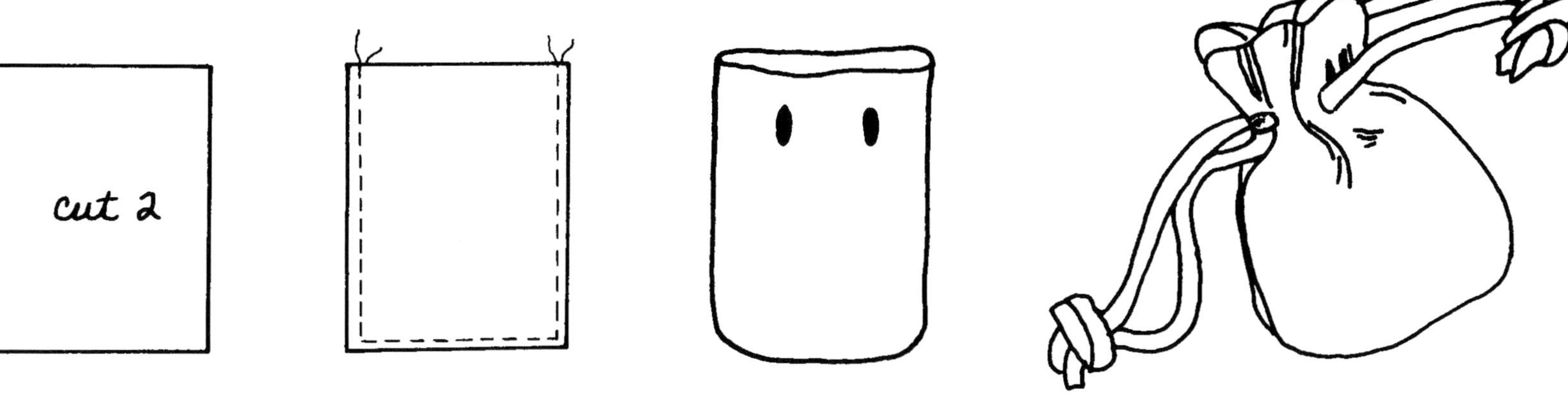

Jump Rope: Rhymes and a Jump Rope

Children have been jumping rope for thousands of years. It is good exercise, great fun, and a good way to improve rhythm and coordination. Long ago jumping rope was a competitive boy's game, a contest to see who could jump the fastest, the highest, and the longest. In the late 1800s, when girls began to play, they added something new — jumping together in groups. Two girls would act as "turners" on either end of a long rope. Other girls would jump in and out while the turners swung the rope either fast or slow as directed by rhymes invented especially for jumping rope. The rhymes helped the turners and jumper keep rhythm, gave them directions on how fast to turn and jump and what special tricks to perform, and gave the game a touch of poetry and humor.

I went downtown to meet Miss Brown.
She gave me a nickel to buy a pickle.
The pickle was sour, I bought a flower.
The flower was red, I bought some thread.
The thread was thin, I bought a pin.
The pin was sharp, I bought a harp.

A Rhyme

We don't know which rhymes the Shaker girls used, but the following rhyme, also chanted when bouncing a ball, makes it easy for you to add your own touches. Fill in the blanks with names, places, and things you know.

A

A my name is ***Anita*** and my sister's name is ***Anna*** and we come from North ***Adams*** with a basket full of apples.

B

B my name is________ and my sister's name is ________ and we come from ________ with a basket full of ________.

C

C my name is__________ and my sister's name is__________ and we come from ________with a basket full of ________.

A Jump Rope

Materials

4 – 5′ of ½″ cotton, nylon, or mountaineering rope
1 foot of rubber garden hose
Large, heavy-duty scissors

Directions

Cut the garden hose into two pieces about 4″ long. The hose will be the handles on the jump rope. Thread the rope through the hose and tie a knot on either end of the hose to hold it in place.

Woodworking

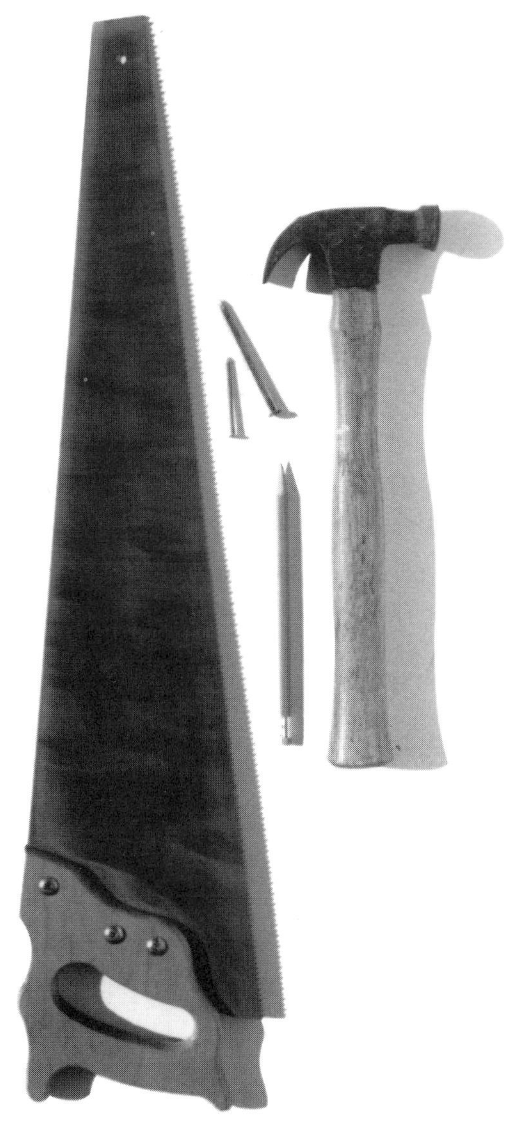

When Nicholas Briggs went to live with the Shakers in 1852, the villages had more or less an equal number of sisters and brothers. Work was divided into traditional jobs for men and women. The sisters cooked and preserved food, worked in the gardens, did the laundry and domestic work, and made woven baskets and cloth. The brothers did the heavy farm work, constructed buildings and small factories called mills, and made furniture and cabinets. Shaker brothers invented two very common objects as they worked with wood: the clothespin and the circular saw. Actually, the idea for the circular saw came from a sister.[3]

Building construction was an important part of the brothers' life. It was their responsibility to comfortably house the huge Shaker families. They used their Shaker values — thrift, simplicity, functionality, practicality, and honesty of purpose — when they designed and constructed buildings. Today many of these buildings are thought to be great architecture and they are preserved as museums. But at the time they were constructed, Shaker buildings were ordinary. As a matter of fact, the dwelling houses were probably considered peculiar by the world's people, because they were more like large hotels than family homes.

The brothers also had to comfortably furnish the dwelling houses. The furniture had to be easy-to-make because they needed so much of it. Even though it was made in great quantity, every piece of Shaker furniture had the

3. Shaker stories passed down from past generations say the circular saw and clothespin were Shaker inventions. It is not a proven fact.

same honesty of purpose, thrift, simplicity, functionality, and practicality. These beautifully crafted pieces of furniture are perhaps what the world best remembers about the Shakers.

After the brothers had furnished their villages, they continued making furniture and sold it to the world's people. Today, fine examples of their furniture may be found in many museums and in private art collections. If you would like to have a Shaker chair in your room, the Shaker Workshops catalog is one excellent source of reproduction Shaker furniture kits. A parent and child can assemble one together and feel the satisfaction the brothers felt when they completed a piece of finely crafted furniture.

Shaker Boy's Ruler

When a new boy arrived in the Shaker village one of his first handwork projects was making a wooden ruler in the woodshop. After wood for the ruler was cut and finished, an iron stamp was used to mark the individual divisions. Whole numbers were stamped on the divisions and all markings blackened for easier reading. The ruler was then varnished and used by the boy when he worked in the village.

Materials

- Piece of pine molding precut to exactly 12 inches
- Fine sandpaper
- Ruler and pencil
- Permanent marking pen
- Danish oil finish and a soft rag

Directions

Lightly sand the pine molding. Carefully transfer the division marks from the ruler to the pine molding with a sharp pencil. Make permanent marks over the pencil lines with a marker. Neatly write the whole numbers under the 1-inch divisions. You may wish to add your name. Pour a little Danish oil finish on the rag and wipe it over both sides of the ruler.

Candleholder

Materials

- 2 feet of ½-inch-thick pine
- Half-dozen 5-penny common nails
- 10-penny common nail
- Hammer
- White glue or glue gun
- ½" auger and clamp
- Saw
- Pencil and ruler
- Compass
- Fine sandpaper
- Danish oil finish and soft cloth
- 8" beeswax candle

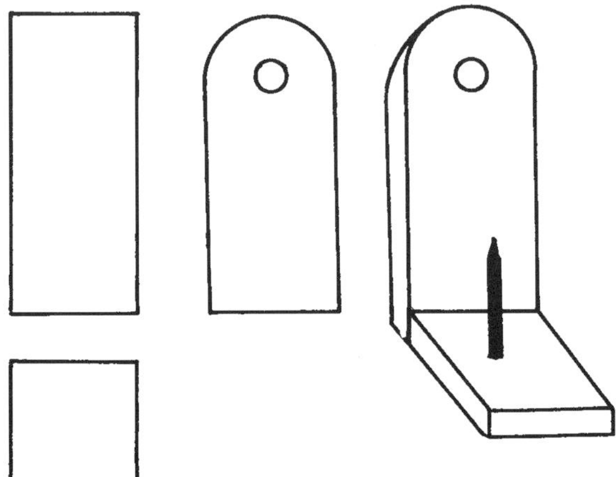

The top of this simple candleholder is the same shape as many objects designed to hang on the row of pegs around the top of Shaker rooms.

Directions *Requires adult assistance*

Step 1 • Measure and cut the wood into two pieces, 5″ x 12″ and 5″ x 5″. Measure 2½″ from the top and sides of one end of the big piece and make a mark with the pencil. Draw a circle with a 2½″ diameter using the pencil mark as the center. Cut away the top half of the circle as illustrated. Clamp the wood to a table and drill a 1″ diameter hole, using the pencil mark as a center. Sand the rough surfaces.

Step 2 • Use the ruler to find the center of the small piece of wood and mark it with a pencil. Clamp the wood to a table and drive the 10-penny nail through the wood at the pencil mark. The protruding nail will hold the candle.

Step 3 • Squeeze a small amount of glue on one end of the small piece of wood. Line it up with the edges of the square end of the big piece of wood. Nail the two pieces of wood together with 5-penny nails. Put the candleholder in a safe place to dry for several hours.

Step 4 • Sand any remaining rough edges on the candleholder when the glue has dried. Pour a small amount of Danish oil finish on the cloth and wipe it over all surfaces of the candleholder. Press the candle down over the nail to secure it to the candleholder.

Birdfeeder

Early Shakers did not believe in keeping pets or in caring for wild animals. This changed in the early 1900s, as we can see from looking at pictures of Shaker cat Theodore Roosevelt Chickenhouse and Shaker dog Dewey. This simple birdfeeder can be used to feed wild birds in winter.

Directions

Lightly sand the wood. Use a ruler to find and mark the center of the wood square. Pound the nail all the way through the wood at the center point. Remove about ½ cup peanut butter from the jar and put it in a bowl. Roll the pine cone in the peanut butter. Press the pine cone onto the nail. Cut the rope into four equal pieces and knot firmly together at both ends. Suspend the wood, pine cone up, in the center of the rope, and the birdfeeder is ready to hang.

Materials

- Piece of pine cut to 10" square
- Sandpaper
- Ruler and pencil
- 12-penny common nail
- Hammer
- Large pine cone
- Jar of peanut butter
- Bowl
- 4½' of lightweight rope
- Scissors

Mills and Mill Ponds

The Shakers were a farming society. But they also made everything they needed. Because electricity had not been invented, machines were powered by running water flowing over huge waterwheels. These waterwheels turned the stones that ground grain into flour and cut trees into lumber. Shaker villages were established where power was available from a nearby lake, river, or stream. The Canterbury farmland was of fine quality, but there was no water power. The resourceful Shaker brothers found water many miles away, channeled it to their land, and engineered and built an elaborate system of eight mill ponds that worked the same as a natural river. The eight ponds were connected by ditches and dams that controlled the flow of water from pond to pond. When water was released it flowed over waterwheels and powered the Shaker's small factories, called mills, built next to the water. In the mills, the brothers ground grain into flour and cut trees into lumber. It was said around Canterbury, New Hampshire, "When the Shakers are finished with the water, it is all worn out."

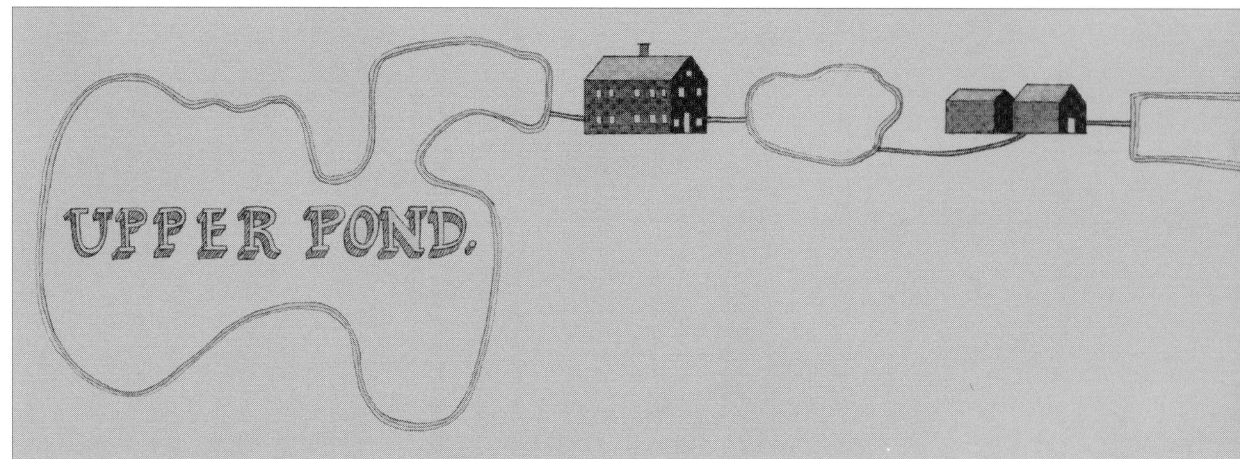

Miniature Mill Ponds

More information about mills and mill ponds may be found at the library in the book *Mill*, by David Macaulay.

Directions *Requires adult approval*

With your parents' permission, find a small place to dig in your yard. Or a trip to the beach will provide lots of sand to dig in. Plan a mill pond system on paper and then build it using a shovel or trowel and stones to make dams. Remember water runs downhill, so make the first pond higher than the second and so on. Turn the hose on low and run it into the first pond. Watch how the water flows from pond to pond. Experiment with moving the rocks and changing the flow of water.

Materials

- Pencil and paper
- Shovel or hand trowel
- Medium-sized stones
- Hose and water source
- A place to dig

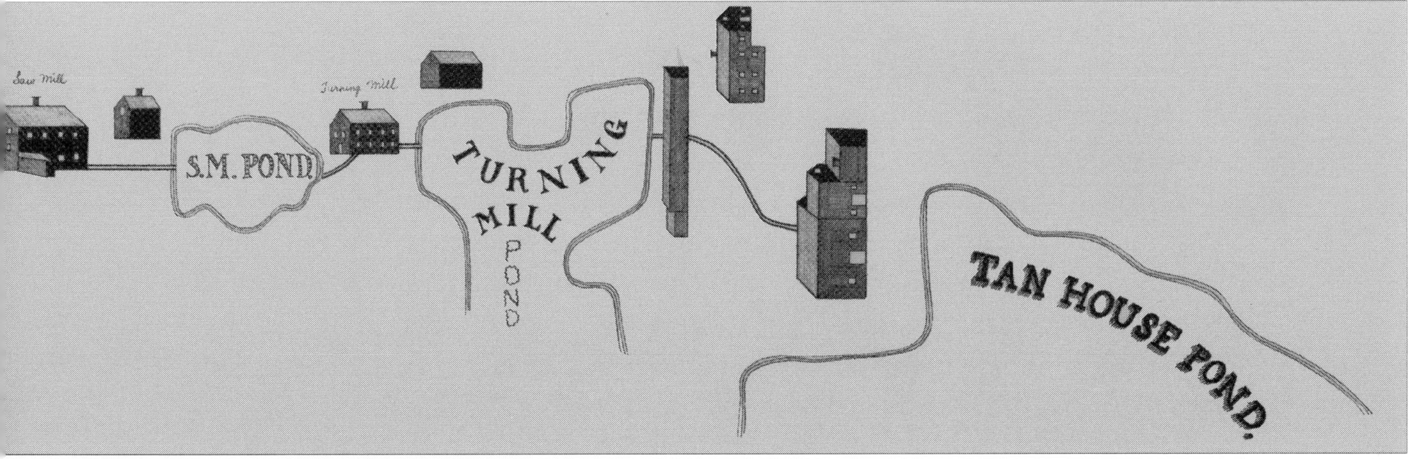

The drawing shows the Canterbury mill pond system. Boys' Island, where Nicholas Briggs and his friends had their garden, is located in the center of one of these ponds. If you visit Canterbury Shaker Village, you can walk out to Boys' Island.

A Broom

Materials

Long straight stick about 3′ long, bark on or off

2 large handfuls of 12″ or longer pine needles

Burlap or heavy colored twine

Heavy-duty scissors

Several 8-penny nails

Hammer

Large bowl

Newspaper

A useful plant in the Shaker fields provided the raw material for another successful industry. Broom corn was made into brooms of the finest quality. One day, Brother Theodore Bates of the Watervliet, New York, Shaker Village was watching a sister sweep with a common round-shaped broom. He thought she was wasting time and effort. Since thrift is an important Shaker value, he made the first flat broom. We don't often credit them with this invention, because the Shakers thought U.S. patents were selfish and preferred to share their ideas with the world.

Nicholas Briggs worked in the Canterbury broom mill. This was a job he disliked because it was dusty and the broom corn hurt his hands. It is hard to find broom corn today. However, long pine needles are a reasonable substitute for real broom corn.

Directions *Requires adult assistance*

Soak the pine needles in warm water for one hour. Remove them from the water and place on newspaper to soak up excess water. Use a hammer to drive two nails into one end of the stick. This will prevent the pine needles from slipping off the stick. Surround the stick completely with one layer of pine needles and tie them tightly in two places with twine. Add a second and third layer, tying each in place. If you like, trim the bottom of the broom with the scissors.

Pouring boiling water over the twine will shrink it and make the broom more sturdy. Ask an adult to help you with the boiling water.

Knitting

Anna Delcheff taught Anita Potter to knit soon after Anita arrived at Hancock Shaker Village. Knitting was hard to learn at first, but as soon as Anita caught on it became her favorite pastime. She found joy in knitting throughout her life.

Knitting is a skill best learned from an experienced knitter. The beginner must first learn how to handle the needles and yarn with enough skill to make the two basic stitches. When the stitches are mastered, knitting becomes fun.

There are several different styles of knitting. It doesn't matter which one you learn. The illustrations will help you remember how to make the two basic stitches when your teacher is not there to help you.

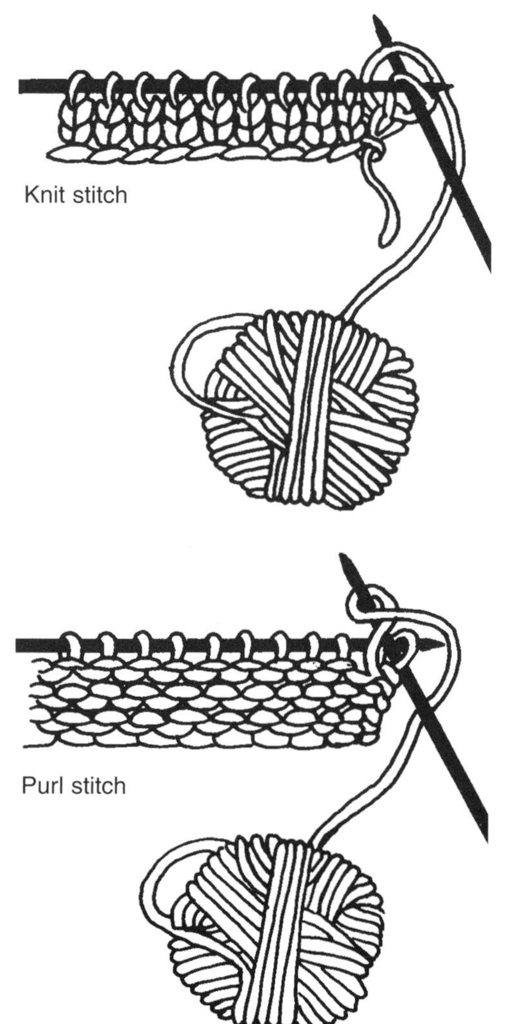

Knitting Vocabulary

Knitting needles • Smooth rounded sticks with pointed ends that are used in knitting. Knitting needles come in different sizes and lengths, and they are straight, circular, or double-pointed.
Casting on • Beginning a piece of knitting by making the first loops on a knitting needle.
Knitting • Pulling yarn through loops on knitting needles called stitches.
Knit stitch • As illustrated.
Purl stitch • As illustrated.
Garter stitch • A piece of knitting with horizontal ribs made by knitting every row.
Stockinette stitch • A piece of knitting with a smooth side and a bumpy side made by alternating one row of knit and one row of purl.
Ribbing stitch • Knitting continuous rows of alternating knit and purl stitches.
Binding off • Taking the stitches off the needle and securing them so they will not ravel.
Finishing • Completing a hand-knitted piece.

A Knitted Headband

This headband covers the ears and may be worn in place of a hat.

Directions *Requires adult assistance*

Cast on 19 stitches. *First row*: Slip first stitch to the next needle without knitting, K1, P1 until you reach the last stitch. Knit the last stitch. You should have two knit stitches at the end of the row. *Second row*: Slip the first stitch to the next needle without purling and continue P1, K1 until you reach the last stitch. Purl the last stitch. Repeat rows 1 and 2 until the headband measures 30″. Bind off. Use the darning needle to hide the tails of yarn at the beginning and end. Lay the finished headband flat on a table. Measure 3″ from the bottom end and mark this with a safety pin. Without moving the headband, turn the bottom end over. This will make a twist in the headband. Pick the headband up, holding the twist in place, and make a loop as illustrated. Stitch the loop in place with the darning needle and a little extra yarn. The loop should be big enough to fit two fingers. Push the other end of the headband through the loop and the headband is ready to wear. The size can be adjusted by pulling the loose end of the headband through the loop.

Stitch

Ribbing made from knit 1, purl 1

Materials

- #8 knitting needles
- 1 skein washable knitting worsted
- Tape measure
- Large darning needle
- Scissors
- Several safety pins
- Sturdy bag for storage of work

A Knitted Tube Headband

Materials

- #8 double-pointed needles
- Scraps of yarn
- Large darning needle
- Scissors
- Sturdy bag for storage of work

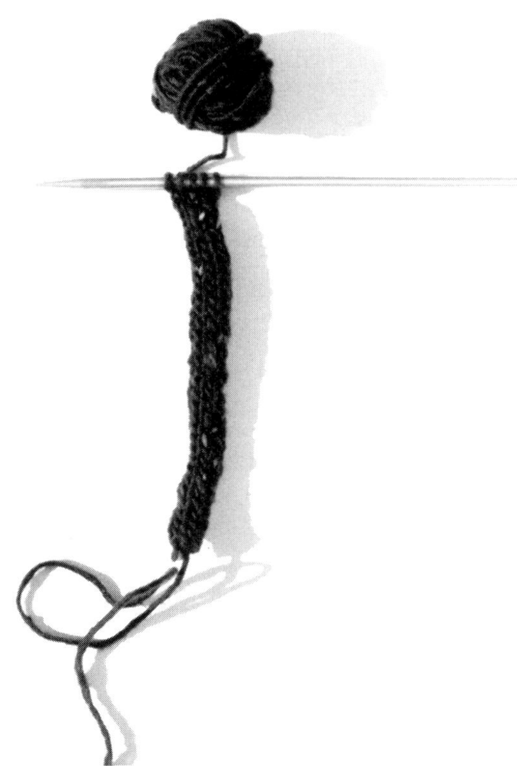

This headband may be knit in one color or in a rainbow of colors by simply changing yarn as you knit.

Directions *Requires adult assistance*

Step 1 • Before you begin your headband, practice this technique until you understand how it works. Cast on 7 stitches. Knit the first row. Slide the stitches across the double-pointed needle to the other end. Without turning the work and beginning at the same side, knit the second row the same way you knitted the first row. Again, slide the stitches across to the other end of the needle without turning the work. Knit the third row the same way you knitted the first and second rows. The back of your knitting will look like a ladder because the yarn is carried across the back of the knitting.

Step 2 • Pull out your practice work and begin knitting the headband, casting on 7 stitches and knitting the same way. Pull the yarn that is carried across the back a little tighter to automatically form a tube. You will not see the ladder at the back of your work.

Step 3 • Knit until the headband measures 30″, changing yarn whenever it pleases you. To finish off the yarn tails from color changes and at the beginning and end of the headband, thread each tail through a darning needle and hide it in the headband. Trim off any excess yarn. Knot the headband together and it is ready to wear.

Knitting Spool and Doll's Rug

The Shaker sisters used spool knitting to make coiled doll rugs and other toys. If you can find a wooden spool, it is easy to make a knitting spool. A search through an old sewing box may uncover several wooden spools. A ready-made knitting spool may be purchased at some special stores that sell toys made in Germany.

Materials

Large empty wooden spool
4 medium-sized round-headed brass nails
Pencil
Hammer

Knitting Spool

Directions

Use the pencil to make 4 evenly spaced marks on one side of the spool. Leaving the top ⅛″ of each nail exposed, pound a nail into each hole.

Doll's Rug

Materials

1 small skein of colorful yarn
Size D crochet hook
Darning needle

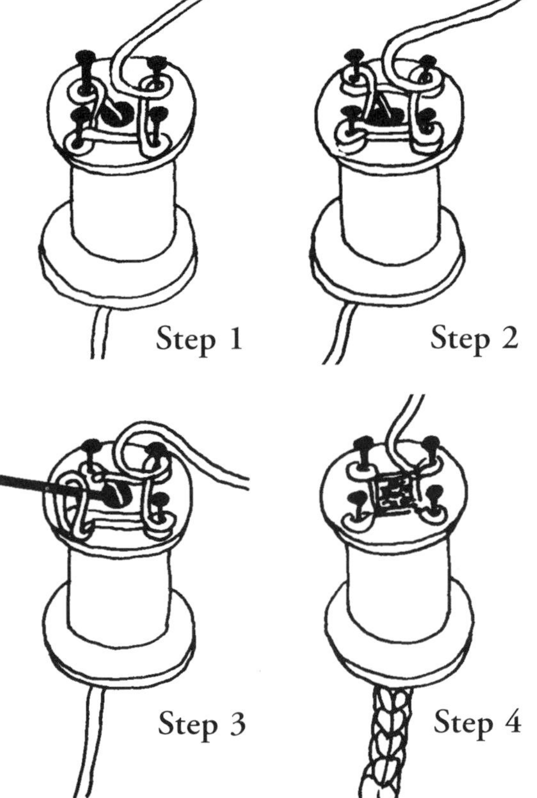

Directions

Step 1 • Unwind a 6″ length of yarn and push it through the hole in the top of the knitting spool. Beginning on the inside of the nail, wind the yarn around each nail one time. Push the row of loops down to the top of the spool.

Step 2 • Wind a second row of loops in the same way.

Step 3 • On one nail, use the crochet hook to catch the bottom loop and pull it over the loop. Do this on all four nails and then pull firmly on the yarn hanging from the bottom of the spool. You have completed one row of spool knitting.

Step 4 • Continue knitting a row and pulling the bottom until your knitted tail or cord is 20″ long. Finish off the cord by slipping one loop over the next until you have a stack of four loops. Cut the yarn from the skein and pull the end through the last loop.

Step 5 • Thread the darning needle with yarn. Coil and overcast stitch the cord to make a doll's rug. Hide any remaining tails of yarn by pulling them through the rug with the crochet hook.

Cross-stitch and Fancywork

Cross-stitch was the most popular form of needlework in the early days of our country. Young girls learned patience and skill in working with their hands when they stitched a sampler. The letters of the alphabet and the shapes of animals, plants, houses, and even tiny people were constructed from rows of neat stitches, each one shaped like a tiny square.

Because early Shaker families had over one hundred brothers and sisters, all of the laundry, even the handkerchiefs, had to be marked with the owner's initials. The young Shaker girls helped with this task, and it was necessary for them to learn to cross-stitch the letters of the alphabet. In later years, the sisters used cross-stitch on their fancywork.

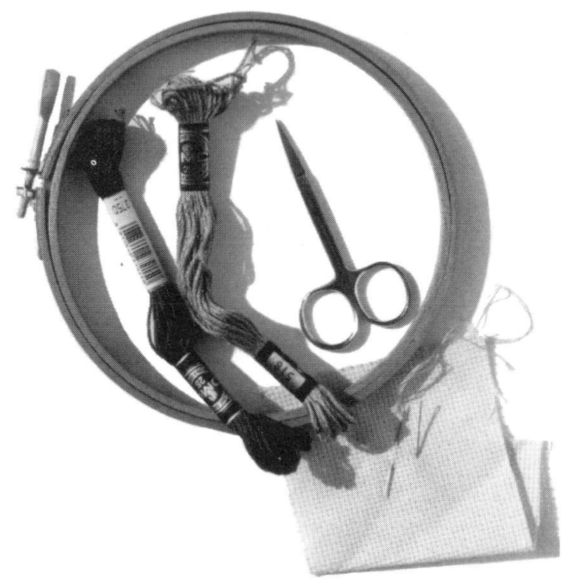

Fancywork objects such as sewing boxes, doll clothes, pincushions, needle cases, baby clothes, washcloths, pot holders, and fir balsam pillows earned extra money for the sisters. These fancy goods were sold at stores in the Shaker villages. And, once a year, the sisters packed their handwork in trunks and traveled out into the world to sell it. Skillfully crafted and lovely to look at, the Shaker fancywork was easy to sell to the world's people.

The following sewing projects have been simplified. The Shakers were skilled workers and even the simplified projects may be too difficult for you to do on your own. You will probably need to work on them with adult assistance. You may wish to use a sewing machine in place of handsewing. Before purchasing new materials for the projects, look around the house with a parent for materials you have on hand. Remember, the Shakers were very thrifty. They wasted very little.

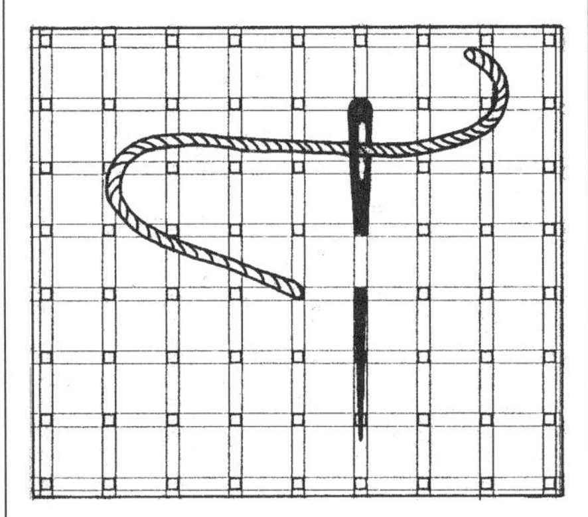

Step 1 ● To begin one stitch, bring the needle up in the lower left hand corner of the first square and insert in the opposite corner of the same square.

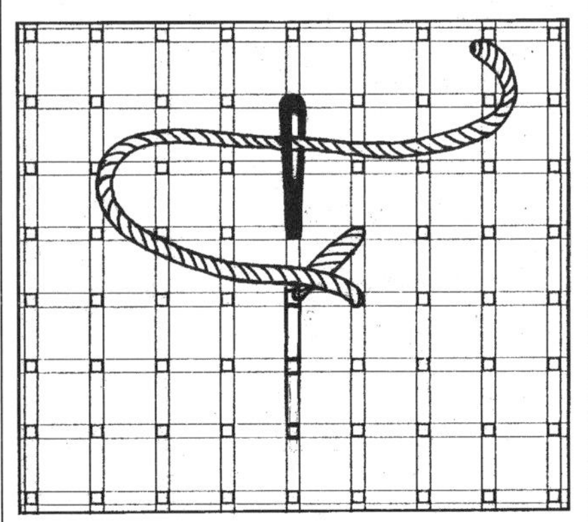

Step 2 ● To complete one stitch, bring the needle up in the lower left hand corner of the same square and insert it in the upper right hand corner.

Cross-stitch Vocabulary

Fabric ● Special fabric is required for the beginning cross-stitcher. It is evenly woven in a pattern of tiny squares. Holes in the corners of each square guide the placement of the needle when making the stitches. This fabric, called Aida cloth, comes in several colors and may be purchased at needlework stores or from needlework catalogs.

Thread ● One-hundred-percent cotton, six-strand embroidery floss is the correct thread for cross-stitching on Aida cloth. You may buy it at novelty stores, needlework stores, some craft stores, and from needlework catalogs.

Needles ● #7 embroidery-crewel needles are best for cross-stitching.

Making a cross-stitch ● The cross-stitch is composed of two diagonal stitches, equal in length, that are worked one over the other from the opposite corners of a square as illustrated. All stitches in a piece of cross-stitched embroidery should cross over each other in the same direction.

Beginning and ending ● When you begin stitching, let 2″ of thread hang loose at the back of the cloth. Catch this thread two or three times with your first stitches. Neatly trim off the excess thread. When you finish the first length of thread, run it under the last four or five stitches on the wrong side of the cloth. Neatly trim off the excess. Begin and end each new thread in the same way. (See page 107 for illustrations.)

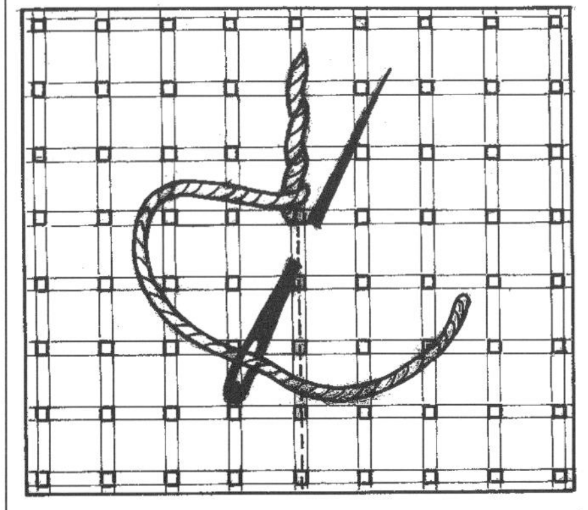

Backstitch

The backstitch is used to show the antennae and legs on the worker bee (see activity on page 108), and to define the windows on the dwelling house in the sampler (see page 110).

Work from top to bottom. Bring the needle out one square from the start of the line to be covered. Insert the needle at the starting point and pull it through two squares down and so on until you finish the line.

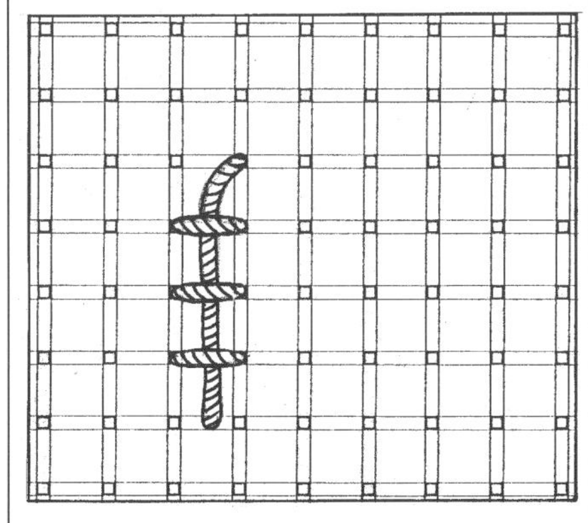

Beginning

When you begin stitching, let 2 inches of thread hang loose at the back of the cloth. Catch this thread two or three times with your first row of stitches. Then neatly trim off the excess. The illustration shows the back side of the cloth.

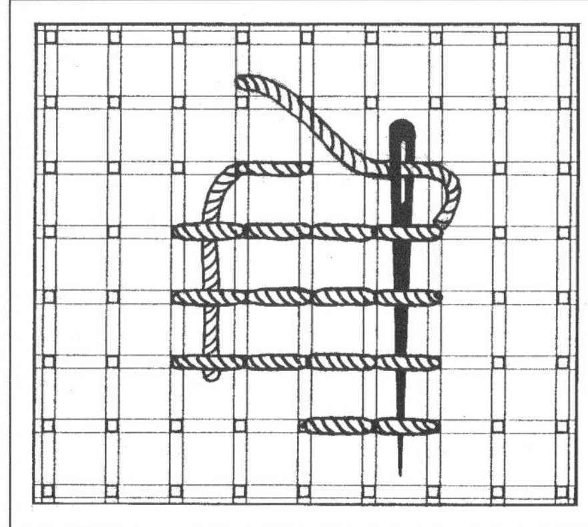

Ending

When you finish the first length of thread, run it under the last four or five stitches on the wrong side of the cloth. Neatly trim off the excess. The illustration shows the back side of the cloth.

Worker Bee Cross-stitch and Pincushion

Materials

- White or yellow Aida cloth, 6" x 6"
- Six-strand embroidery thread to match the colors in the key
- #7 embroidery needles
- Small scissors
- Small box for storage of work
- Ruler and soft pencil

Color key

- ■ Black
- □ Yellow
- ☒ Gold

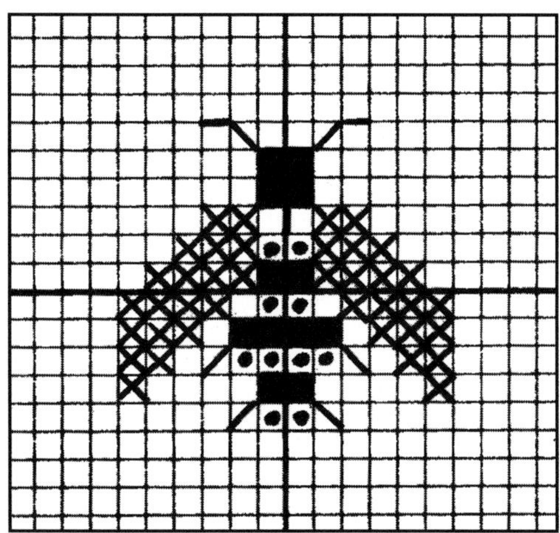

The bee is a symbol of busy Shaker communal life. Honey, the product of the bee's labor, is sweet and symbolizes the sweetness of Shaker life.

Use the graph as a map to count out the colored stitches. The key will tell you the colors represented by the different symbols.

Cross-stitch

Directions

Use the ruler to find the center of the cloth. Mark the center with a light pencil mark. Find the center point, marked with a black circle on the graph. Begin stitching at this point. You must count the stitches on the graph and copy them exactly onto the cloth.

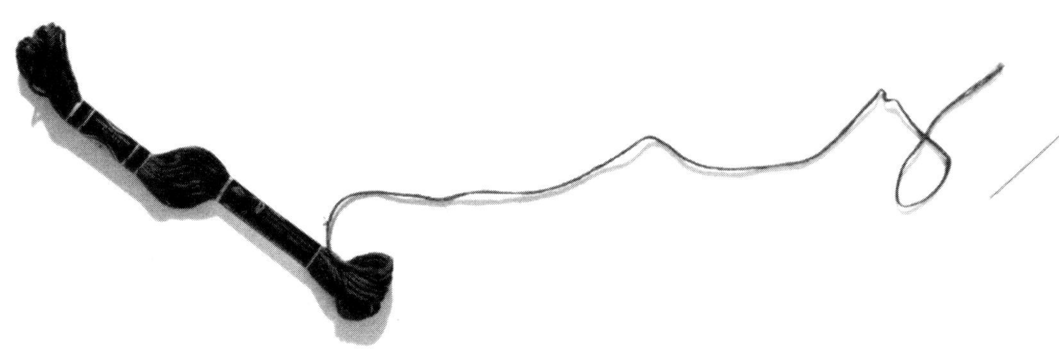

Worker Bee Pincushion

Pincushions were popular fancywork items. Although other shapes were used, many were shaped like a velvety tomato.

Directions

Step 1 • Hand-wash the finished cross-stitch in warm water and mild soap. Squeeze out excess water with a bath towel. Air dry and press lightly with an iron.

Step 2 • Trim the cloth to 5″x 5″, centering the cross-stitch in the square. Pin the two squares of fabric together, right sides facing inside. Because sand sharpens needles and pins, it is the best filling for a pincushion. Machine sewing is the best way to keep the sand from leaking out of the pincushion. Sew the two pieces of fabric together, leaving a 1″ opening on one side.

Step 3 • Use a small funnel to fill the cushion with sand and hand-stitch the opening together.

Materials

- Finished Worker Bee cross-stitch
- 5″ x 5″ square of gold velveteen or good-quality felt
- Needle and gold thread
- Pins
- Sewing machine
- 1 cup clean, fine sand
- Small funnel
- Scissors
- Bath towel
- Iron

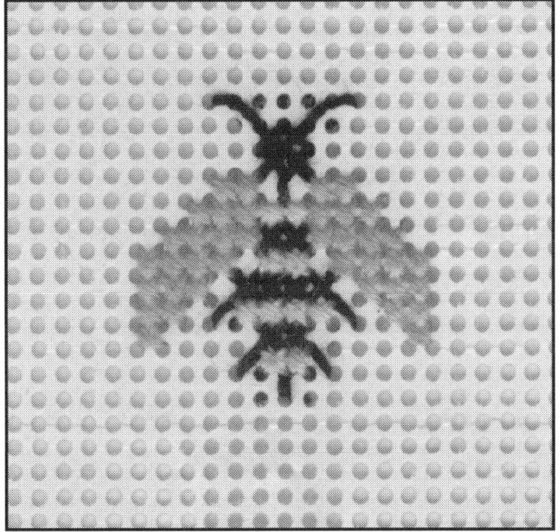

Color key

- ☒ Burnt orange
- ☐ Pale yellow
- ● Forest green
- • Grey blue
- ■ Black

Cross-stitch Sampler

Shaker brothers drew a charming and colorful pictures of their villages. This sampler, showing a Shaker dwelling house with a comet flying overhead, was inspired by drawings made by Charles F. Priest (Harvard, Massachusetts) and Joshua H. Bussell (Poland Hill, Maine).

This is an ambitious cross-stitch project, but if you have the patience to finish it, you will have a treasure to keep for many years.

Use the graph as a map to count out the colored stitches. The color key shows the colors represented by the different symbols. The illustrations show how to fill in large areas with the same color stitches. You will use this technique to stitch the dwelling house, dove, and trees.

Directions

Use the ruler to find the center of the cloth. Mark the center with a light pencil mark. Find the center point of the pattern and mark it with a light pencil mark. Begin stitching at this point. You must count the stitches on the graph and copy them exactly onto the cloth.

Materials

- Punched paper for cross-stitch or white Aida cloth, 12" x 12"
- Six-strand embroidery thread, 1 skein for each color in the color-key
- #7 embroidery needles
- Small scissors
- Small box for storage of work
- Ruler and pencil

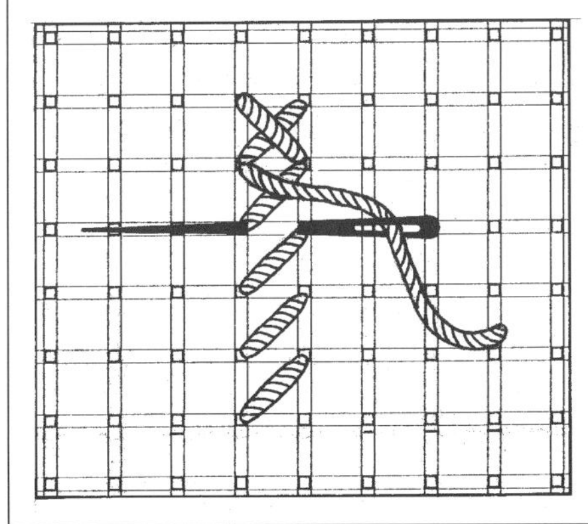

The illustration shows how to fill in large areas with the same color thread.

Doll-sized Dorothy Opera Cloak

Materials

¼ yard red cotton fabric, medium weight
1 yard red satin ribbon, 1″ or wider
Red thread
Pins and sewing needle
Scissors or rotary cutting tool
Sewing machine (optional)
Ruler

Around 1890 Eldress Dorothy Durgin of Canterbury crafted a cloak in an elegant new style. The Canterbury Shakers recognized the merit of the Eldress's design and advertised the cloak. Soon the Eldress's beautiful hooded cloak became high fashion for women of the world. Even the wife of the president of the United States, Mrs. Grover Cleveland, owned a Dorothy Opera Cloak in dove gray.

The Dorothy Opera Cloak pattern is one of the few Shaker inventions that has not been offered to the world. The Sabbathday Lake Shakers have the original pattern and it may still be possible to order one from them. This doll's version has been simplified to make it easy for a beginning sewer. This project will require adult assistance.

Directions *Requires adult assistance*

Step 1 • The first set of measurements are for an 8-inch doll, the second for a 13-inch doll, and the third for an 18-inch doll. Cut a piece of fabric, (8″ x 10″) (13″ x 13″) (18″ x 18″) for the body of the cloak. Cut a second piece (3″ x 10″) (4″ x 13″) (5″ x 18″) for the shoulder cape and casing.

Step 2 • Lay the larger piece of fabric flat on a table and pin the smaller piece to it (3″) (4 ½″) (6 ½″) from the top as illustrated.

Step 3 • Machine- or hand-stitch the pieces together using a ½″ seam.

Step 4 • Turn and press the cape down.

Step 5 • Machine- or hand-stitch ⅝″ from the seam to form the casing.

Step 6 ● With right sides facing each other, machine- or hand-stitch the top of the cloak together to make the hood. Shape the back of the hood by machine- or hand-stitching a T-shape across the back.

Step 7 ● Pull the ribbon through the casing and gather the cloak on the ribbon until it fits the doll.

Step 8 ● Fit the cloak on the doll and trim to ankle length. You may wish to round the corners slightly. Press under raw edges and stitch a hem by hand or with a sewing machine. If necessary, gather the hood together in the back at the top with a few hand stitches.

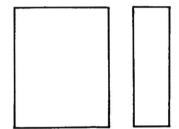

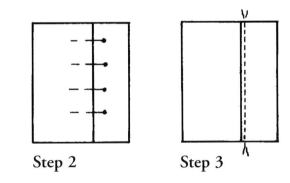

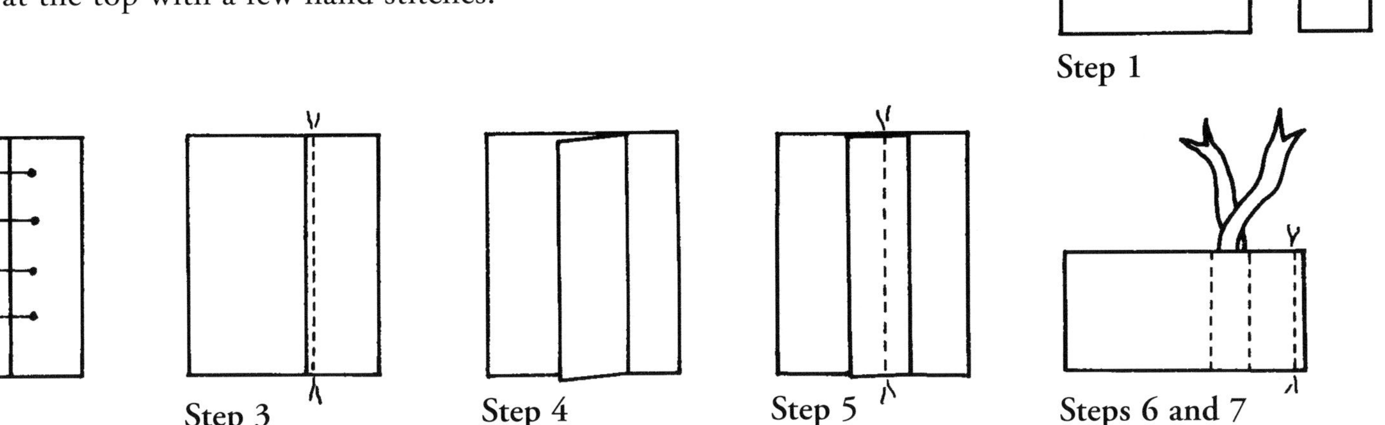

Quantity • 3 pillows

Materials

- Several fresh short-needle pine branches
- ½-yard transparent fabric
- Matching thread
- Pins
- Scissors
- 1½ yards fancy ribbon, 1″ wide
- Hand-sewing needle or sewing machine

Fir Balsam Pillows

Making fir balsam pillows has been a popular Shaker craft for many years. The Sabbathday Lake Shakers still make and sell fir balsam pillows.

Any cotton fabric scraps can be used to make the pillow coverings. Fancy pillows made from transparent fabric let you see the texture of the pine needles inside. Red, green, gold, or silver fir balsam pillows are pretty enough to give as a gift at Christmas time.

Directions

Step 1 • Cut the fabric into three 6″x 12″ pieces.

Step 2 • Fold the first piece of fabric in half and machine- or hand-sew a seam on the long side. A French seam will prevent the fabric from raveling.

Step 3 • Fold one end of the fabric back 3″ and hand-stitch it in place to make a deep hem at the top of the pillow.

Step 4 • Machine- or hand-stitch across the bottom. Form corners for the bottom of the pillow by stitching diagonally across the ends.

Step 5 • Remove the needles from the pine branch. Turn the pillow inside out and fill it with needles to the line made by the deep hem. Gather and stitch the fabric together at the hemline.

Step 6 • Tie a bow with ½ yard of ribbon to cover the hemline. Trim the edges of the ribbon at a slight angle to prevent raveling.

Villages/Museums/Shopping

Canterbury Shaker Village
288 Shaker Road
Canterbury, New Hampshire 03224
603-783-9511
Village/museum, restaurant, and shop open daily May through October, 10 A.M. to 5 P.M. Call for special events, restaurant hours, and winter hours.

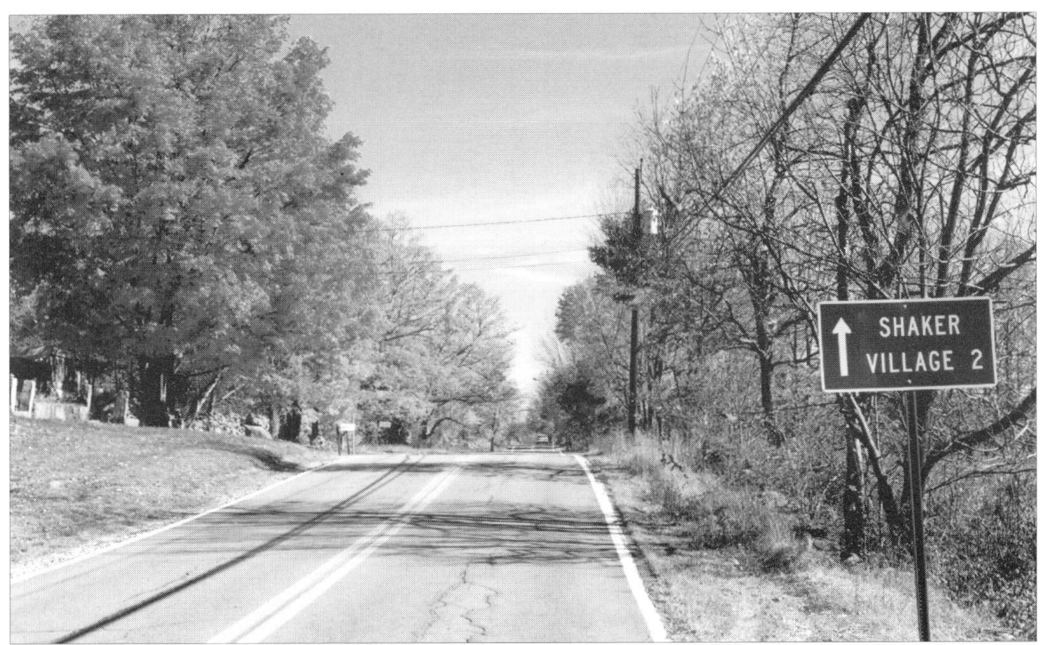

Enfield *(on Route 4A)*
2 LSV
Enfield, New Hampshire 03748
603-632-4346
Village/exhibits, store, inn, and restaurant. Call for hours.

Hancock Shaker Village *(on Route 20)*
P.O. Box 898
Pittsfield, Massachusetts 01202
413-443-0188
Village/museum, shop, cafe open daily May 1 through October 31, 9:30 A.M. to 5 P.M. Call for special programs and winter hours.

North Union/The Shaker Historical Society
16740 South Park Boulevard
Shaker Heights, Ohio 44120
216-921-1201
Museum open year-round, Tuesday through Friday and Sunday, 2 P.M. to 5 P.M. Closed holidays.

Mount Lebanon Shaker Village *(on Route 20)*
P.O. Box 628
New Lebanon, New York 12125
518-794-9500
Village/exhibits and store open daily Memorial Day weekend through Labor Day weekend, 9:30 A.M. to 5:00 P.M.

Sabbathday Lake *(on Route 26)*
RR 1, Box 640
Poland Spring, Maine 04274
207-926-4597
Village, museum, shop, and store open Memorial Day through Columbus Day, Monday through Saturday, 10 A.M. to 4:30 P.M. Closed Sundays.

Shaker Museum and Library
Old Chatham, New York 12136
518-794-9100
Museum, shop, and cafe open daily May 1 through October 31, 10 A.M. to 5 P.M. Call for special events.

Shakertown at Pleasant Hill
3500 Lexington Road
Harrodsburg, Kentucky 40330
606-734-5411
Village/museum, shops, inn, restaurant, and boat trips. Open year-round, 9 A.M. to 6 P.M., winter until 5 P.M.

Shakertown South Union *(on Route 73)*
South Union, Kentucky 42283
502-542-4167
Village/museum, shop, tavern/inn and restaurant open March 15 through November 15, 9 A.M. to 5 P.M. and Sundays 1 P.M. to 5 P.M.

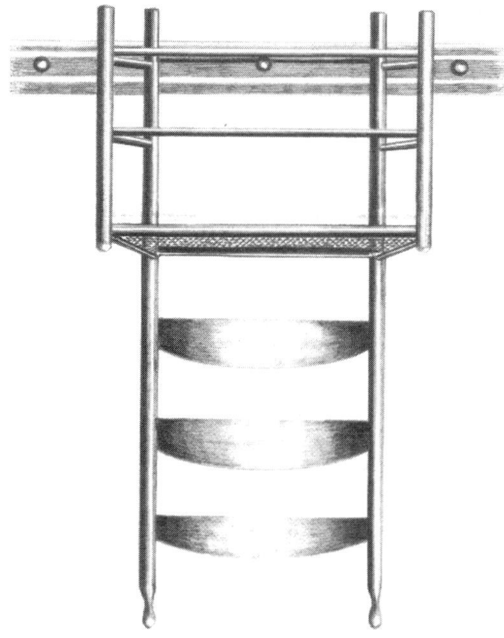

Watervliet/Shaker Heritage Society
1848 Shaker Meetinghouse, Albany-Shaker Road
Albany, New York 12211
518-456-7890
Museum and shop open year-round, Tuesday through Friday, noon to 4 P.M., except major holidays.

Union Village
c/o Warren County Convention & Visitors Bureau
777 Columbus Avenue
Lebanon, Ohio 45036
513-933-1138
Museums, inn, restaurant. Call for hours.

The ***Shaker Heritage Guidebook*** offers a listing of Shaker Public Collections and Libraries throughout the United States and in Great Britain.

Shaker reproductions may be purchased by catalog from
Shaker Workshops
P.O. Box 1028
Concord, Massachusetts 01742
800-840-9121

Shaker herbal products and rose water may be purchased from
The United Society of Shakers
RR1, Box 640
Poland Spring, Maine 04274
207-926-4597

Shaker Glossary

boys' house • Where Shaker boys slept.

boys' shop • Where Shaker boys spent daytime hours.

brother • A Shaker man.

brother's waiting room • A room where Shaker men sat quietly before meals.

caretaker • A Shaker who supervised the care of children.

cleanliness • Free from dirt.

communal life • People sharing everything with each other.

dwelling house • The Shaker equivalent of a family house.

elder • A Shaker man who lead the community with an eldress.

eldress • A Shaker woman who lead the community with an elder.

fancywork • Handcrafted goods such as needle emeries that were sold to "the world's people."

health • Maintaining top physical condition.

kiln • A large oven.

mill • A small factory built along water.

mill pond • Water dammed up to run a mill.

meeting room • The Shaker equivalent of a church.

nay • The Shaker word for no.

needle emeries • Small objects made from cloth, and filled with sand used to sharpen sewing needles.

order • A neat and harmonious arrangement of things.

perfection • One of the Shaker ideals; synonymous with beauty.

perfect life • Living as though in heaven while still on earth, perfection without defect, complete.

trustee • Members of Shaker families who took care of family business.

trustee's office • The place of business in a Shaker village.

retiring room • A Shaker bedroom.

retiring time • Time spent in solemn silence to prepare for a religious service.

Shaker a plate • To clean all traces of food from a plate.

simplicity • Sincerity and freedom from unnecessary decoration.

sister • A Shaker woman.

stint • An assigned task for a specified time.

square • A shaker table setting for four people.

thrift • Not wasteful.

union meetings • Informal occasions when Shaker men, women, boys, and girls could socialize in small groups.

Victrola • An early record player.

world • Everything outside the Shaker villages.

world's people • People who are not Shakers.

yea • The Shaker word for yes.

Bibliography

Andrews, Edward Deming and Faith. *Visions of the Heavenly Sphere: A Study In Shaker Religious Art.* Charlottesville, Virginia: The University Press of Virginia, 1969.

Barrett, Marilyn. *Aggie, Immies, Shooters, and Swirls: The Magical World of Marbles.* Boston: Little, Brown and Company, 1994.

Briggs, Nicolas. Forty Years a Shaker. *The Granite Monthly* (1921): N.p.

Bremness, Lesley. *The Complete Book of Herbs.* New York: Viking Studio Books, 1988.

Brewer, Priscilla J. *Shaker Communities, Shaker Lives.* Hanover, New Hampshire: University Press of New England, 1986.

Canterbury Shakers. *Gentle Manners: A Guide to Good Morals.* 1823. Reprint, Canterbury, New Hampshire: Shaker Village, 1978.

Cole, Joanna. *Anna Banana: 101 Jump-Rope Rhymes.* New York: Morrow Junior Books, 1989.

Cone, Ferne Geller. *Classy Knitting: A Guide to Creative Sweatering for Beginners.* New York: Atheneum, 1984.

Editors. *Simple Gifts: 25 Authentic Shaker Craft Projects.* Pownal, Vermont: Storey Communications, 1990.

Faber, Doris. *The Perfect Life: The Shakers in America.* New York: Farrar, Straus and Giroux, 1974.

Gordon, Beverly. *Shaker Textile Arts.* Hanover, New Hampshire: University Press of New England, 1980.

Johnson, Pauline. *Creating with Paper: Basic Forms and Variations.* Seattle: University of Washington Press, 1958.

Linsay, Eldress Bertha. *Seasoned with Grace: My Generation of Shaker Cooking.* Woodstock, Vermont: The Countryman Press, 1987.

Miller, Amy Bess, *Shaker Herbs, A History and Compendium.* New York: Clarkson Potter Publishers, 1976.

Miller, Dr. M. Stephen. *A Century of Shaker Ephemera.* New Britain, Connecticut: Dr. Steven M. Miller, 1988.

Murray, Stuart. *Shaker Heritage Guidebook: Exploring the Historic Sites, Museums & Collections.* New York: Golden Hill Press, Inc., 1994.

Mahoney, Kathleen. *Simple Wisdom: Shaker Sayings, Poems, and Songs.* New York: Viking Studio Books, 1993.

Macaulay, David. *Mill.* Boston: Houghton Mifflin Company, 1983.

Ott, John Harlow. *Hancock Shaker Village: A Guidebook and History.* Hancock, Massachusetts: Shaker Community, Inc., 1976.

Paige, Jeffrey S. *The Shaker Kitchen.* New York: Clarkson Potter Publishers, 1994.

Patterson, Daniel W. *Nine Shaker Spirituals.* Old Chatham, New York: The Shaker Museum Foundation, Inc., 1964.

Pearson, Elmer R. *The Shaker Image.* Boston, Massachusetts: New York Graphic Society and the Shaker Community at Hancock, Massachusetts, 1974.

The Shakers. *Catalog of Fancy Goods.* Sabbathday Lake, Maine: Shaker Village, 1910.

Sprigg, June. *By Shaker Hands.* Hanover: The University Press of New England, 1990.

———*Shaker Design.* New York: Whitney Museum of American Art in association with W. W. Norton & Company, 1986.

Sprigg, June and Larkin, David. *Shaker: Life, Work, and Art.* New York: Stewart, Tabori & Chang, 1987.

Stein, Stephen J. *The Shaker Experience in America.* New Haven: Yale University Press, 1992.

Thorpe, Anita Potter. *Shaker Girl.* N.p, n.d.

Turning Mill Pond Trail. Canterbury, New Hampshire: Shaker Village, 1993 (pamphlet).

Vadnais, Andrew for Hancock Shaker Village. *Oral Interview with Anita Potter Thorpe.* N.p., n.d.

Van Kolken, Diana. *Introducing the Shakers: An Explanation & Directory.* Bowling Green, Ohio: Gabriel's Horn Publishing Co., 1985.

Whitcher, Mary. *Mary Whitcher's Shaker House-Keeper.* Hancock Massachusetts: Hancock Shaker Village, 1882. Reprint. N.d.

For photographs and illustrations I am grateful to the following:

Photograph on front and back cover, © David Duncan;

on pages iii, 1, 3, 6, 35, 36, 38, 39, 40, 41, 46, 47, 48, 49, 51, Hancock Shaker Village;

on pages 4, 5, 14, 28, 29, 30, 32 left, 66 right, Canterbury Shaker Village;

on pages 23, 42, 80 (seed packet shape), Shaker Museum and Library;

on page 34, The United Society of Shakers;

on page 9, The Library of Congress;

on pages 22, 26, 31, 32 right, 44, 60, 63, 66 left, Stephen Miller;

on pages iv, 7 top, 10, 15 bottom, 16, 17, 19, 27, 33, 37, 96, 97, 117, June Sprigg Tooley;

on pages 58, 59, 62, 106, 107, Linda Brownridge;

on page 75, James and Graham Pulliam;

on page ii, Per Pearson;

on page 2, E. Ray Pearson;

on pages 7 bottom, 8, 15 top, 18, 20, 21, 24, 25, 43, 45, 50, and all pages not otherwise identified, Kathleen Thorne-Thomsen with photographic prints by Manuel Martinez at the Darkroom Workshop.